Beyond the Paradox of Being Human

A Panoramic Experience

Mark Waller, Ph. D.

WingSpan Press

Printed in the United States of America

Published by WingSpan Press, Livermore, CA
www.wingspanpress.com

The WingSpan name, logo and colophon are the trademarks of WingSpan Publishing.

Cover Photo by Mark Waller

ISBN 978-1-59594-141-1

First edition 2007

Library of Congress Control Number 2007921297

Mark Waller(909) 614-1218
The Waller Group, Inc.
4195 Chino Hills Pkwy. PMB 611
Chino Hills, CA 91709-2618

mail@markwaller.com
www.markwaller.com

Foreword

As the publisher of *Pathways for Spiritual Living Magazine*, a periodical that explores the integration of Western psychology and Eastern spirituality, I have read literally hundreds of books in these subject areas and have reviewed many dozens of them for the magazine. While I am often delighted and edified by my reading of the psychological and spiritual works currently on the market, I must admit that I am rarely surprised. Many of these books are quite repetitive in theme, if not in specific content.

Then I read Mark Waller's *The Paradox of Being Human*. I was literally blown away by his insight and originality. In this remarkable book, Mark has been able to integrate such complex psychological concepts as first- and second-order change, attachment theory, the physiology of the limbic system and cerebral cortex, the theory of parts and subpersonalities, and original sin (to mention only a few!) into a comprehensive and panoramic perspective of the human spiritual condition. Then he puts these amazing insights into language that is both simple and accessible to the general reader. Mark's central and guiding insight is that human existence is paradoxical by its very nature. Think of it this way. There are two kinds of people in the world: seekers and finders. Seekers are those people who are always looking for the next spiritual experience or the next existential insight into the meaning of life. They are never satisfied. As George Eliot writes, "The golden moments in the stream of life rush past us, and we see nothing but sand; the angels come to visit us, and we only know them when they are gone." Finders, on the other hand, are awake to their current experience. They seem to be fairly content with life as it is and go about their days just enjoying the ride. Now here's the problem: seekers can *never* be finders (please take your fingers out of your ears and stop humming). Seekers are so attached to their identity as seekers that actually finding what they want or desire would involve a frightening loss of identity. It would literally ruin everything for the ego. So they keep on seeking, ignoring everything they *do* have, and remaining in denial about the absolute futility of their search.

This reminds me of the story of the Zen master who told his students that they must meditate with focused attention and conscious intention and that they must desire enlightenment more than anything else in the world. The next day, of course, he told them they could never possibly become enlightened as long as they desired it. (Do you ever wonder why more Zen masters don't get shot?) Mark Waller's insight is essentially the same: we can either seek or we can find. We just can't do both.

I hope I have stimulated your curiosity enough so that you will read this book with focused attention and conscious intention. I can tell you right now that it won't fulfill your seeking, because nothing ever will. But it just might teach you how to live your life exactly as it is. I leave you with these words of Alfred D. Souza:

"For a long time it had seemed to me that life was about to begin--real life. But there was always some obstacle in the way, something to be gotten through first, some unfinished business, time still to be served, a debt to be paid. Then life would begin. At last it dawned on me that these obstacles *were* my life."

Richard G. Young, Ph.D.
Author of *Paths of a Prodigal* and *A Ticket to Athens*
Publisher, *Pathways for Spiritual Living Magazine*
Director, Center for Contemplative Christianity
Clinical Director, Pathways Counseling Center

Table of Contents

Introduction

The knowledge outlined in this book can lead one to a new sense of power, control, and confidence in situations. By staying in the Meta-Self role, as explained within the text, power comes from not trying to get it. Confidence comes from not needing to know. Control comes from not wanting it. Recognition comes from being uninterested in it. Acceptance comes from accepting *self* first. We get what we need by not having expectations. We protect ourselves by becoming vulnerable.

The more one tries to control and protect the more power they give away. Every reaction gives away power and life force. Paradoxically, one must learn to stay within one's self to join more fully with the world. As soon as you react, you give away any power you have in the situation and become victims of circumstance. By staying present and becoming curious about one's own internal process as well as the process of others, awareness can be brought to the situation and create new options and opportunities.

For years, I wanted to achieve my full potential as a human being. I wanted psychic powers. I wanted to work miracles of healing. I believed that deep inside all of us, there was untapped potential. I wanted to tap mine. Then I wanted to help others tap theirs.

It seemed reasonable to me that there had to be some formula to do all of this, like six steps to perfection and power, or something like that. There was a time when I believed I just had to hypnotize myself effectively enough. I was religious for a while. Then later I thought the answer must be in meditation or stroking crystals.

In my forties, I came smack up against the real problem. There was darkness inside of me with another agenda going its own direction. I had to admit that I wasn't some "New Age" type of guy. I was angry, depressed, and sullen. I had been for much my life.

I had worked on my potential. I had gone to all the "right" workshops and read the right books. Nevertheless, nothing prevented my life from collapsing - status, relationships, and finances all evaporated. I was forced, because of my pain, to look at my soul instead of my aura. What I found was not pretty. An incident, which happened a few years ago, brought this to my attention in detail. I was a consultant. I gave speeches, taught classes, and wrote books. The conference I was attending was held at the Sheraton Universal City near Hollywood.

I had been particularly upset at the organizers and had made no effort to hide my frustration. In my opinion, the conference had many flaws, not the least of which was the failure of giving me a prominent enough role. I was only dimly aware of my huge need for recognition at that time. Everyone else's failings were my constant focus.

I'm a large man at six foot, four inches, and at the time, I weighed a little over three hundred angry pounds. My vehicle of choice in those days was a full-sized, black Bronco. On any given day, I would careen violently down the freeways of LA. I loved to loom up behind other drivers like their worst nightmare from a Stephen King novel, and intimidate the person in front me until he got "the hell out of my way!"

A colleague from across the country attending the same conference sat me down one afternoon. "Mark, you're an angry person. Life is too short to be so angry."

I stammered a little, my eyes bugged out in shock, I must have attempted an unconscious gulp down my suddenly dry throat.

"Let me tell you a story, Mark. I was angry just like you once."

Tell me a story he did. It was a horrible story. One of those stories no one ever wants to hear. The man's eyes filled with tears as he spoke, but he didn't stop until the story was finished. There had been a tragic accident. He had lost his child. What followed was the gradual disintegration of his life, divorce, and loss of career. I could see in this man's heart he would never stop feeling guilty and never forgive himself.

"And that's how I learned life was too short. If I had only known what would happen, I would have lived differently. I would have let go of my anger and tried to find a little more joy along the way."

The story was overwhelming. I had two beautiful daughters. I could not comprehend the pain of losing either one of them. He and

I parted that afternoon, and I never saw him again. I did talk to him on the telephone once to thank him. Even as unconscious as I was in those days, I realized this man had been willing to re-experience his own great pain so that I might experience an epiphany. It was a gift, for I knew he was right. I had to change.

My growth process took years. Along the away, I squandered my marriage. I lost my home. I even worried that I was so unlovable that I had lost my daughters.

It was a full moon the night my wife of twenty-one years moved out. She had rented a house in the same town. We lived in La Canada at the time. The first residents of the area had come from the Midwest to cure the ravages of asthma, believing the dry air in the Pasadena area had curative powers. Then it was known as the Glen behind the Verdugo Mountains. That's what La Canada means, the Glen.

My house was at 2,000 feet up the southern slope of the San Gabriel Mountains. From my patio, I could see over the San Rafael Mountains the entire Los Angeles basin. The last 4th of July we spent in the house, we had been able to see no less than 24 fireworks displays. On a clear day, you could see Catalina Island, planes landing 35 miles away at L.A.X., and tall buildings in Newport Beach nearly 60 miles away. It had a view!

Even the perspective of that "view" did not stop the inevitable disintegration of my life. I had stayed in our home the day she moved out for purely practical purposes. The bankruptcy hearing was scheduled weeks away, and I knew I would not be evicted for some time. This worked out nicely since I had no money. Two years before, my consulting practice had grossed over two hundred thousand dollars. The month of our separation, I had to borrow money for my estranged wife to survive.

There were days, years actually, when all I knew was fear. How was I going to survive? Were my dreams dead? I would acknowledge my fear in the hope that dealing with it would somehow produce growth. Though it took many years for me to sort out my interior reality and to understand my anger, I had a transformational experience during those lonely months. That experience laid the initial seeds for this book. I will share that experience with you shortly. In that moment of enlightenment, I was able to see the path to my healing.

This process of discovery has been moving and spiritual for me. However, this is not a book about religion, or metaphysics. It is a book about personal change and development. If you have any strong emotional reactions along the way, take note of them. They are important signposts marking the areas of your life waiting for transformation.

The human condition is paradoxical. By living in the paradox, we give up abundant life and all its richness. Peace and harmony are available, but not inside the paradox. This book is about The Paradox of Being Human, and how to move beyond to the freedom that is our heritage. It explains the human condition in a new way and offers a way out of this trap. We have had the ability inside us all along to experience our full potential. The paradoxical quality of human nature starts almost immediately in each life. By the time we're grown, we act as if we have no choice but to pursue life in this paradoxical manner. Read this book, analyze your own life, observe your behavior, and discover your own path to freedom.

Chapter One

Life's First Contradictions

Researchers know that all people have a primary relationship that leads to either a secure or insecure attachment style. If a person is lucky enough to be one of the 60 percent of children who were securely attached, the rest of their life will be a much more bearable circumstance. If a person, however, was one of the unfortunate 40 percent of children who has an insecure attachment style, intimate relationships will be more difficult. However, there is hope. The pathway to healing the pain and rage leftover from the attachment experience is now clearly understood and will be laid out in the following chapters.

We all want to experience our true potential. We all want to have a life where we are connected and fulfilled, alive and vibrant. The Russian teacher and mathematician P.D. Ouspensky called that "remembering yourself." He said that we are all asleep, meaning that we are all acting like mechanistic automatons. We're only pretending to be awake. The goal in life, according to Ouspensky is to awaken and remember who you really are.

What puts us or keeps us asleep? What is it about the human condition that produces such slumber that we cannot even remember who we are? We are not born to be asleep in this way. The process of sleeping-while-seeming-to-be-awake is a gradual one. It starts from nearly the first moments of our lives.

Mark Waller, Ph.D.

CASE 1: JOSE' AND MARIA

Maria is complaining that her husband is emotionally unavailable. When he comes home, he just watches TV, and he doesn't really care about her.

"Jose', what about that?" I ask. "Are you unavailable?"

"She's always hitting me and screaming at me. Sometimes I have to grab her to get her to stop. It worries me. If I accidentally scratch her, I can go to jail."

He's right. He could go to jail. She could go to jail. When the police arrive on a domestic violence call, it's like a lottery to see if the real attacker goes to jail. However, as I was listening to him, an alarm bell went off in my head. I turned to Maria. "Is that right? Do you scream at him and hit him?"

She appears chastened and nods. "I don't know what comes over me. I just get so angry."

If I'm going to help this couple, there is a vital piece of information than I need. I question her about her background, her family. Her father was an alcoholic, but he was happy and available. They spent a lot of time together. She says he was fun, and they used to play a lot. Her mother, on the other hand, wasn't around much. When she was, she was cold and unapproachable.

"Let's pretend you are two years old for just a moment, Maria. I know it sounds crazy, but just play along. So, you're pretending to be two years old when suddenly your mom walks into the room. You look at her. What's the first thing that goes through your mind? Just say the first thing that pops up."

She looks toward the door as if imagining her mother standing there. Quickly, without thinking, she looks back to me and asks, "What am I supposed to do?"

For an instant, I think she didn't understand my instruction. Then I realize that I initially missed the meaning of her response. I got my answer. There was no response to seeing her mother. "Okay, mom's here, so what am I supposed to do?" The entrance of mother into the room prompted a non-reaction. Now I know where her rage comes from – insecure attachment.

Attachment: The Bonding that Explains Behavior

After birth, our world is tiny and includes only ourselves. Soon we become aware of another being outside ourselves. At first, we think it's really an extension of us. We become aware of this "other" through touching, nursing, a familiar scent, and the sound of a voice. When we smile, she smiles. We gurgle and she tickles our belly. We do not yet even know if there is a "who" that is tickling, but our world is larger now. It includes this "other" we interact with, usually our mother. Gradually it can include our father. We are very resourceful; however, we can bond to whoever happens to be handy as a primary caregiver: a nanny, an aunt, or a sister if no parent is available. Which primary person is there to care for us is not the issue when it comes to bonding. What is critical is what happens in that relationship. Bonding is a

2

vital developmental process. Who is not the issue, the quality of the process is the issue. The earliest process that can establish contradictions in our lives is called *attachment* otherwise known as bonding.

Attachment is a behavioral control system that is instinctive in infants. Inside our brain at birth, we have a set of innate behaviors designed to assist us in attracting someone larger than ourselves to insure our survival. We are pre-wired to do little things with our faces in an attempt to get any kind of response from that other person out there. The control that the infant is attempting to exert is to assure the closeness of the caregiver. The baby smiles, the caregiver responds. When the baby does anything, hopefully the caregiver reacts with joy.

The infant instinctively realizes that the attachment behavior has been successful when closeness to the primary caregiver has been achieved. We learn to recognize all those crazy faces that mom and dad make as they look into the crib or hold us. We need those big folks close because we are physically helpless at this point.

Think of the human infant as a naked, baby animal. Contrary to how we might want to see ourselves, this is how we start life. This very vulnerable being has to have some kind of system to protect itself. The only thing available is somehow to attract the attention of a larger, stronger being that can provide protection. Babies use an innate system of facial expressions, noises, reaching, pointing, and later following behind the caregiver to elicit a response from the caregiver. The response they want is proximity. Proximity means needs will be met, needs for food and protection. Babies also signal for a response from the caregiver by crying, babbling, and later calling.

The primary purpose of the attachment process for the child is to get physical needs met. First among them is to be fed. This fits into the overall strategy of staying alive, being safe, and not becoming part of the food chain. The bond of affection that results from attachment can be thought of as a secondary gain. Little babies are trying desperately to control the physical closeness of their primary caregiver through a complementary dance of movements, which include facial expressions, arm movements, and noises.

Babies need to know that their attachment behaviors will bring the caregiver to them. **Since attachment is about survival, it predominates over all other behavioral systems.**

As we grow, we develop systems for communication, for courtship and sex, and for other ways of expressing who we are in the world. All of our social systems have our experience of attachment as their foundation. Even if we're involved in some other behavior or focused on some other priority, activation of the attachment behavior system will supersede all other behavior. This is vital to our understanding of the human condition, even in adults.

We do not outgrow attachment needs, nor do we abandon attachment behaviors as we age. The brain builds upon this early learning. Scientists call this "generalization." Like a seed in the ground, our early experiences of bonding extend up, branch out, and color our perception of the social world even as it becomes increasingly complex. Our attachment needs and the way we attempt to meet them become complex too.

A child's needs are not complex. They are immediate. The child may die if it doesn't maintain the proximity of a larger, stronger caregiver. Failure of the baby to achieve the goal of attachment results in the terror of death.

In fact, experts on childhood development know that without an attachment figure such as a mother or father, or other caregiver, babies will wither and die. The clinical label for this is *failure to thrive*. In the state of California, if an infant fails to thrive, parents can serve hard time for this violation of the state penal code on child abuse.

A number of things activate attachment behavior. Should the caregiver be at an unacceptable distance, the attachment control system is triggered in the brain. Babies scream loud when their mothers leave. Discomfort, hunger, and other conditions also trigger the attachment control system. If the baby's environment is stressful, such as too hot or too cold, or unfamiliar - the child will seek proximity to the caregiver by acting out movements, sounds or facial expressions to bring the caregiver closer. The drive towards attachment behavior is at the very core of our existence.

Most important, however, is the behavior of the caregiver. A healthy relationship between infant and caregiver is complementary. They're not the same behaviors, but they are intertwined. The infant is constantly care-seeking and the caregiver is constantly care-giving.

Should the behavior of the caregiver suddenly shift from a pattern familiar to the infant, the infant will immediately activate a system of control behaviors in a desperate attempt to reestablish the complementary behaviors.

Failure to gain the response the child is seeking results in insecurity, possible danger, and the infant perceiving a threat to his or her life. Continuous frustration of these attempts by the infant to control the caregiver's response results in a complex emotional reaction that is a mixture of terror and rage.

Attachment Styles

The process of attachment is most critical during the first three years of life. The infant uses the attachment figure, usually the mom, as a secure base from which to explore and internally pattern the world. At the first sign of trouble, the infant bolts to mom for cover. Gradually, children can tolerate longer absences and/or distance from the parent. This process of learning develops internal neural networks or brain patterns of the child in relation to the caregiver, which the child will use for reassurance when the caregiver is absent.

Developmental researcher, John Bowlby, was the father of attachment theory. He studied infants and their mothers and was the first to document the power and effectiveness of the attachment process. Later, Mary Ainsworth another researcher in child development expanded Bowlby's original research. Ainsworth and her colleagues used a laboratory technique called "the strange situation" to observe the interaction between infants and their mothers. This involved removing the mother from the child and then reuniting them.

The researchers lead mothers and children into a strange room. The mothers stayed with their children while the children became accustomed to their surroundings and explored a little. Just when they got comfortable, the mothers were escorted out of the room leaving the children alone. The infants became scared, sad, and upset, but after a while, they settled down, and then the mothers returned.

The behavior on reuniting was closely observed. The observations fell into four categories:

First, there were those infants labeled "securely attached." These infants greeted their mothers with smiles and wanted to be close. A second group was labeled "avoidant." These children either ignored their mother's return or resisted contact with their mothers. The third group was labeled "ambivalent." These children at first sought contact with the mother, but then resisted the contact angrily. The final group of children showed a mixed or disorganized version of avoidant or ambivalent behaviors, or they displayed random and/or seemingly purposeless behavior. Avoidant, ambivalent, and disorganized attachment styles are all lumped into a term the researchers called "insecure attachment."

CASE 2: DERRICK AND SYLVIA

The case of Derrick and Sylvia is an excellent example of attachment styles. An incident they related to me points out what can happen when attachment goes awry. They had been sitting one Saturday morning in a restaurant eating breakfast. The previous evening had been absolutely a wonderful time for the two of them together. Sylvia was looking at Derrick over her breakfast plate still experiencing warm feelings from the night before. Quite unexpectedly, Derrick said to her, "I can see you're looking at those men that are sitting behind me. I bet you would like to go to bed with them. Wouldn't you?"

Sylvia was shocked. "You're crazy! How many times do I have to tell you I don't think those kinds of things?"

"That's bullshit. You're a liar. You're always thinking about other men."

"You're jealous. You have no reason to be jealous of me."

Derrick was now raising his voice in anger. "Jealousy? That's bullshit. You've lied to me before, and you're lying to me now."

The rest of the day did not go well between Derrick and Sylvia. Jealousy of this magnitude is the result of unmet attachment needs.

It is easy to see that Derrick, from the above example, is insecurely attached. His behavior, rage and jealousy, indicate that he has no internalized patterns for a trustworthy caregiver.

The term "self-in-relationship" describes these internalized patterns. In other words, self-in-relationship is how a person "knows" how to act when they are with someone else who is perceived as relatively important.

It is important to understand that an individual's attachment style is re-enacted in most relationships as they continue to age. His or her internal patterns of self-in-relationship will make each intimate partner an attachment surrogate as Sylvia is to Derrick. Without a healthy first experience of self-in-relationship, a person will have a reservoir of terror and rage that, when activated by an "attachment crisis" can be directed at any current attachment figure. The behavioral response will fall into one of the categories mentioned above; secure, ambivalent, avoidant, or disorganized. Adult attachment styles are an outgrowth of those labels and have been categorized as secure, fearfully preoccupied with relationships, avoidant, and dismissing. Insecurely attached partners have relationships that are often volatile and unstable.

CASE 3: TONY AND LIZ

Tony had just been released from jail for assaulting Liz and had been mandated to go to 52 weeks of therapy for "anger management." Tony had been born in American Samoa. At the age of 18 months, his mother and father had moved to the United States to build a better life. Tony was left behind with his grandparents for three years. During those three years, he never saw his parents. When he was four and a half, his parents sent for him and he arrived in the U.S. to join them only to discover a one-year old sister who had been born while he was separated from the family.

Liz, had parents who divorced when she was four years old. Even while she was still in her mother's womb, her parents' relationship was stormy. Frequent fights often lead to violent arguments, and even some physical blows on the part of both mother and father.

Violence can not only be the source of insecure attachment, but it subjects a child to an extremely chaotic and unpredictable environment. The result of this in later life is Post-Traumatic Stress Syndrome, P.T.S.D.

P.T.S.D. produces a child that is in a constant state of arousal and hypervigilance. Insecure attachment and Post-Traumatic Stress Syndrome are not the ingredients of successful relationships.

Tony's insecure attachment and the fear of abandonment that resulted from the loss of his mother during the attachment phase explains his rage. Tony and Liz's relationship was volatile because it was based in fear and distrust due to the insecure attachment styles developed with their primary caregivers. Their lives were characterized by instability and out of control impulses. As a result, their sporadic attempts at getting help through therapy were short lived. They arrived for sessions late, missed sessions, and left therapy altogether as soon as they felt even the slightest relief from their turmoil.

If someone falls into the category of "securely attached" this doesn't mean that all is well. Attachment is not a perfect process. Moreover, attachment styles are reinforced through time. Therefore, attachment is two-dimensional. One dimension is the degree of security around attachment, while the other is the degree to which life experience reinforces the original experience.

The securely attached child who activates attachment behavior and whose mother responds in a consistent and complementary fashion lives in a predictable world. The child achieves the goal of proximity to the mother. The mother-child interaction encourages the child's independent exploration of the environment. This process is vital if the child is ever to separate from the mother and achieve what psychology labels as "individuation," or to become a human being emotionally separate from the mother. The child uses the mother as a secure base from which to learn more about the world and stay safe. This leads to what we consider normal cognitive development and emotional maturity. In other words, secure attachment promotes confidence in a stable and safe world, which promotes smart and happy brains in children. The importance of this process for child development cannot be overstated.

Since attachment styles are laid down the first three years of life, infants don't actually think in simple declarative sentences. It's easy for adult brains to understand their experience if we put it in language as I have done in the previous paragraph. In fact, babies have no autobiographical memory during most of the attachment phase, which will be discussed later. Since there is no autobiographical memory at the time of attachment, the neural pathways of learning laid down in our brains must be of some other "stuff." This means that adult perceptions are not the stuff that instigates attachment behaviors even later in life.

Developmental theorist Jean Piaget labeled the learning that takes place in the first 24 months of life as "sensorimotor." In other words, the internal patterns of learning are not about words, but how words are said, tones of voice, a look in the eye. Sensorimotor means senses and movements. Early learning is primitive. One doesn't remember what was said, but how it was said.

This explains why one partner in a relationship will often say after a fight, "I don't know what I said to set him or her off."

No wonder this person is mystified. What triggered the combative response from the partner was sensorimotor in nature, not adult communication. Kids with insecure attachment or those exposed to domestic violence, unpredictable or threatening homes grow up with brains adapted to a world that is unsafe, chaotic, and distressing. Studies have shown that boys, for example, will see hostility and aggression in a facial expression or an off hand remark. It may be a look or a tone of voice that is the trigger. This leads to an aggressive and often violent response. For girls from the same environment, similar sensorimotor perceptions may result in emotional shut down and withdrawal even in mildly threatening circumstances. These children are not focusing on verbal cues. Without the knowledge that this behavior comes from sensorimotor cues, no wonder an intimate partner would say, "I don't know what I said to him to set him off."

Case 4: Mark and Laurie

Something similar to this was happening between Mark and Laurie. Laurie had all of the classic symptoms of Posttraumatic Stress Syndrome. She would wake up in the middle of the night frightened and not be able to go back to sleep. Her early memories were sketchy, but it seemed she learned fear from her mother and shame from her father. He left Laurie and her mother when she was quite young and began to have an affair with Laurie's aunt. This act became a lifelong source of humiliation for Laurie.

Mark, on the other hand, had a father who abandoned the family when Mark was three years old. His mother alternately sought emotional gratification from her young son, and raged at him when she was disappointed or depressed. He grew up within an attachment style that compelled him to take responsibility for everyone else's feelings. At the same time, he was always scanning for the inevitable explosion.

When they finally came to see me to try to repair their relationship, she was nearly always openly angry, and he was a cowering, quivering blob. Neither one could explain what cues set them off. She would "blame" him for not showing her love. He would "blame" her for attacking him.

When the cues for conflict are sensorimotor, like Laurie and Mark, we have little choice but to blame, distort, and rationalize. Since the actual source of the trigger is so primitive and deep within early learning, people invent causes that seem logical even though not true. In Laurie and Mark's case, this displayed itself as a "he said, she said" argument where both alternately corrected the other person's version of events and tried to set the record straight.

Case 5: Jim

Jim is an example of an insecurely attached child. He has a mother who uses him to fulfill her own need for love and closeness. Jim's father is either physically or emotionally unavailable, and, consequently, his mother has only Jim, her child, with which to become emotionally fulfilled. It is a huge temptation to view the child as an emotional resource. The mother follows her son, Jim, around and encroaches on the exploration process. Consequently, Jim has a growing fear of being engulfed and smothered that becomes mixed up with the instinctual drive for proximity to his mother. At the same time, this constant proximity of his mother may result in baby Jim's actually fearing the exploration process. Consequently, Jim may prefer to be near the comfort of his mother instead of going through the developmental stage of overcoming the fear of being autonomous from his mother.

What if Jim's mother, instead of emotionally needy, was over protective? She would still follow Jim around constantly interfering with the exploration process but may not be available emotionally. The attachment process in this case sends the message to Jim that he is incompetent, and that the world is an extremely dangerous place. At the same time, Jim's bonding needs are ignored.

What if, in another scenario, Jim cannot get his mother to respond in complementary fashion to his attachment behavior? In this case, his mother may even punish him for attempting proximity.

The famous experimental psychologist, Harry Harlo and his wife, M.K. Harlo, spent years investigating the bonding behaviors of Rhesus monkeys. They set up many situations in which the "mother" was evil, noxious, or abusive. This was done using crude wire replicas of a mother monkey. Regardless of the obstacles to bonding, the baby monkeys clung to these "surrogate" mothers even more tenaciously. This type of behavior is consistent with that of abused children whose attempts at attachment have been met with disinterest and neglect, or punishment. No matter how difficult their childhood most will defend the abusive parent and deny the abuse itself.

One client, Phil, carried an enormous amount of fear of "failing to do the right thing." In a short period of therapy, it became clear that his mother ridiculed him constantly as a child. We discussed the impact of the attachment process. Just like those monkeys clinging to their wire mothers, Phil refused to come back to therapy because I was "blaming his mother."

Sally was an even more extreme case. She was riddled with anxiety left over from a shocking home life. During one incident, she had witnessed her mother forcing her older brother to eat his own vomit. She refused to return to therapy because I had characterized the mother's behavior as "child abuse" and psychotic. She stated she didn't want to say anything bad about mom.

There is also a type of mother who is sometimes there and sometimes not there when the child's proximity-seeking behaviors are triggered. This mother may be an alcoholic or a drug addict. She may be the victim of domestic violence or postpartum depression. If she does not respond consistently, her child will create an internal representation of the world as inconsistent. "Sometimes you will be safe and sometimes you won't be."

All of these babies; Phil, Sally, Jim, are experiencing unmet attachment needs. When these needs are frustrated and the child faces the possibility of death, the response within the child is rage and hatred.

To understand the human condition, it is vital that one realizes that this anger is a primitive defense against feelings of abandonment and fears of danger to the point of death. In effect the infant, if he or she could talk, is saying, "You won't come when I need your protection. Therefore, I'm going to die. I hate you!"

The story of attachment is more than just the quality of bonding between an infant and his or her primary caregivers. It's also about brains and development. Parenting, it turns out, is a more awesome responsibility than has ever before been realized.

Chapter Two

Bonding Equals Babies Brains

It all starts in the Limbic System. The brain has three basic parts: the R - Complex, sometimes known as the reptilian brain; the Limbic System, sometimes referred to as the mammalian brain; and the neo-cortex also called the cerebral cortex.

1. The R - Complex is that part of the brain that is defined mainly by the brain stem and lower parts of the brain. Its responsibility is keeping us physically alive. It is in charge of basic bodily functions like body temperature, respiration - much of what we think of as the automatic functions of our physical body.

2. The Limbic System is deep inside of the brain, and is made up of the Fomix, the Septum, the Hippocampus, the Mammilary, and perhaps most importantly, the Amygdala. The Amygdala is like grand central station for emotions and instinctive behaviors.

3. The neo-cortex is where all those functions that separate us from the animal kingdom take place. For our purposes, the most important parts of the neo-cortex are the frontal lobes. The frontal lobes take up most of the area above our eyes in our foreheads. Think of the frontal lobes of the neo-cortex as the adult brain, where we plan and make choices and decisions.

The Limbic System is Where We Live

The Limbic System is the part of the brain where we have all of our instincts for self-preservation. This is intimately tied to the parts of the brain that learn the skills of sensorimotor perception. After just a few weeks in our mother's womb, the Limbic System starts dramatic development. This part of the brain is literally shaped, wired up, through experience. Even while we are still inside of our mothers, the Limbic System is learning. It learns about the environment inside mom and outside of mom. Loud sounds, bright lights, rock and roll music, and arguments all penetrate and effect primitive learning. The effect of the outside world on mom changes her body chemistry. These changes affect the development of the Limbic System. For example, any sudden changes in adrenaline that might be caused by violence, fear, or shock has an impact on the tiny brain of the infant growing inside. The impact may be only momentary as far as the baby's Limbic System is concerned, but if these conditions are repeated or are continuous, long-term brain development will be affected.

The reason some researchers call the Limbic System the mammalian brain is that it is where we learn all of our instinctive, self-preserving behaviors just like our animal counterparts. After birth, and through the first three years of life, the Limbic System literally explodes in size, number of neural connections, and complexity. Learning causes the brain to wire in the patterns of that, which is learned as billions of neural connections called synapses. An infant receives so much stimulation that the brain creates these connections and then prunes them at a furious pace.

In the first few months of life, the infant's brain will grow 20 fold in connections. A two-year old's brain has twice as many connections as an adult's brain. One can scarcely imagine what kind of learning it takes a child to walk and talk. The amount of activity at the cellular level inside the brain has to be enormous to accomplish these kinds of basic, fundamental, developmental tasks.

However, the infant is not just learning to walk and talk. As we stated in the last chapter, the infant is also learning to bond through the process of attachment. The Limbic System, this center for learning self-preservation strategies and automatic life saving behaviors, has to adapt to an entirely different type of environment than that of early man when people lived in caves. Back then the Limbic System came in very handy. Early man needed to be able to flee from Saber-Tooth Tigers. He needed to duck when a threatening shadow appeared overhead. He needed anger to protect his territory. He needed fear to save his life. Back then, man lived in the wild, and he needed to learn special automatic emotions and behaviors in order to survive.

Today most people no longer live in the wild. Instead, people live in *wild families*. One's survival strategies are about how to survive one's parents and family. Emotional re-activity is no longer about territory or survival, it's about patterns of relating and the expectations associated with those patterns.

Even in the wild, personal survival depended on the relationship with one's attachment figures. Baby humans can't just jump up and run away from grizzly bears like baby rabbits or fawns. Therefore, children from early times have been highly tuned in to even the minutest cues they receive from parents. Research has shown that they are especially sensitive to those parenting styles that foster insecure attachment.

Now, rather than learning about relationships and how they relate to our physical survival in a wild and primitive world, we learn social survival along with everything else we need to learn as children. Unfortunately, our social brain, the frontal lobes of the neo-cortex, won't start dramatic wiring until we're five to seven years old, and they don't fully mature until we are near high school graduation. Therefore, the learning of attachment, secure or insecure, takes place in the Limbic System - the old mammalian brain, the self-preserving, emotionally reactive part of us. Thoughtful decisions are not made here. The Limbic System acts without thinking!

There has been an enormous amount of research done on kids exposed to domestic violence. An unpredictable and threatening home life has a huge impact on physiology and behavior. It's as if these children's "fight or flight" systems have been permanently activated. They have tense muscles, trouble sleeping, and rapid heart rates. In essence, their Limbic Systems have been wonderfully adapted to survival in a prison camp.

Most of us are not particularly surprised that child abuse leaves emotional as well as behavioral scars. However, what we fail to understand is that those scars are the way the Limbic System is shaped. Researchers now have evidence that severe stress in childhood changes limbic structures in the brain. The old cliché that a child is like a lump of clay is true. The Limbic System is that lump of clay. The byproducts of childhood adaptations reside in the Limbic System. In other words, the Limbic System adapts itself to the environment in which we are raised.

Attachment then, is the process of forming the limbic structures according to the world it expects to find out there. The bottom-line is emotional re-activity, which is the Limbic System's stock in trade. Attachment experiences and abuse or stress added to social learning equals the Limbic System and ways of perceiving. The result is the sum total of an individual's emotional re-activity and patterns of relating.

Coincidentally, the Limbic System finishes full neural development at about the same time the attachment phase of social development has ended. This synchronicity of inside vs. outside is the foundation of our lives. As adults, we will act out our childhood survival strategies metaphorically in relationships, especially intimate ones. Even in our careers, they will be the organizing principles of our lives.

Two Developmental Questions

Amy and Dick are a couple who came to see me. One of her pet peeves about Dick was that whenever she writes a check and fails to enter the balance, Dick would go ballistic. Dick claimed that Amy didn't understand the consequences of losing track of their checking account balance. He expressed that tracking the money is his responsibility and without her good bookkeeping practices, he would lose control and worry about a financial disaster.

Amy, on the other hand, interpreted Dick's uptight attitude toward the checkbook as reflecting on her competence. Whenever he tried to reason with her about this issue, she lashed out at him for putting her down.

In my experience, this is a classic conflict regarding the underlying, fundamental emotion that drives each of them. The problem is these are different emotions, and they are hidden below their awareness. Dick is feeling fear and Amy is feeling shame.

Each child must answer two developmental questions for itself as he or she grows up. These are metaphorical questions, not literal questions. They are the basis from which the Limbic System will organize itself as it grows and expands, and eventually connects with higher functioning parts of the brain. Therefore, the answers to these questions are extremely important.

The first developmental question you may be able to guess based on our discussion about attachment. This question is "Am I safe?"

When the child asks this metaphorical question, implicit in it is the question, "will I live or will I die." Also implicit in the question is, "if it's unsafe for me to be here, what should I do to survive?"

If the answer to the question is, "no, the world is not safe," you can imagine what emotion the child must feel - fear. In many ways, the word "fear" is an understatement. Perhaps we should use the word "terror." What's important for us to understand is that the child who gets this "no" answer organizes his or her Limbic System around that early feeling of fear/terror. Remember, the Limbic System helps us adapt and form self-preserving strategies. For the child who gets the "no" answer, the world is a scary place from that point on. Developmentally the child builds on this foundation for all of its other learning. The child is *fear based*, and that fear is the organizing principal of their lives.

How does the child get a "no" answer to this metaphorical, developmental question? If the child is conceived and born into a violent, chaotic, or unpredictable environment, the chances of learning that the world is an unsafe, dangerous place are excellent. The single most common example of a fear-based environment is that of the alcoholic family. Alcoholism usually goes hand in hand with all of the other ingredients of unstable homes. In fact, 80 percent of all violence in homes is associated with alcohol abuse.

Some of us become fear-based through the silent messages and injunctions we receive from our parents as youngsters. It's not unusual for me to hear the following comment from a fear-based person. "There was nothing unusual about my childhood; I came from a "white picket fence" background."

This is not surprising. We don't have to come from a horrendously abusive background to get a "no" answer to the first developmental question of our lives. Remember how sensitive children are to all of the nonverbal cues that they get from parents. They get the message whether it comes to them directly or indirectly. And remember these answers aren't given just once. The answers are situational, attitudinal, and emotional spheres in which the child learns to adapt.

Each child personalizes the fear that he or she feels. One person might be afraid of losing control of their environment. Another child might be afraid of losing love or approval. For some, it's the fear of abandonment. Each fear-based infant learns that fear has a special personalized twist that results from the conditions that come with that "no" answer. Each fear-based person has his or her own brand of fear.

What if the child gets a "yes" answer to this vital developmental question about personal safety? They get this "yes" answer because they are raised in a more stable and consistent environment. On the other hand, perhaps they get subtle cues that they interpret as safety. Now they move on to ask the next developmental question. That question is, "okay, the world is a safe place. *Is it okay for me to be me?*"

The answer for all of us is "no." The answer we get is more in the form of, "yes dear, as long as you are a good little boy." In other words, we get a conditional answer. This answer says you're not okay just the way you are. You're only okay if you act or behave in a certain way. The result of this is *shame.*

Shame is a global assault on ones sense of self. Shaming comes in many forms. Saying, "you're a bad boy," is a form of shame. It produces a feeling of "I'm not acceptable." Physical beating can be interpreted as shaming if the messages that go with the beating are value judgments about the child. The range of emotions that shame produces run the gamut from feeling unlovable to assuming you're unfit for human contact.

I once had a client in group therapy whose mother repeatedly slapped him in the face in front of others. He grew up with an overwhelming sense of *shame.* At the same time in the same group, there was another man who, when he was seven years old, learned to sleep fully clothed. He learned this because it allowed him to awaken from a sound sleep when his stepfather started to beat him. The boy could then race outdoors for safety. This man was *fear-based.* This shows how the same form of abuse seen through different lenses of perception produce shame on one hand and fear on the other. Even fear-based people end up being shamed.

As with the previous example of Amy and Dick, it's easy to see that Amy is shame based. Her Limbic System is organized around the feeling that she is somehow not good enough. Dick, meanwhile, is fear based. He is desperately trying to control the world around him in order not to feel the fear inside of him. Ironically, it is my experience that fear-based people tend often to end up in relationships with shame-based people.

As we shall see, the paradox of the human condition starts with these feelings of fear and shame. The Limbic System, once it gets the message of fear or shame from the attachment process, must adapt to it. This adaptation creates struggle in each of our lives until awareness gives us new choices. Helping you to find this awareness is the purpose of this book.

The Beginning of the Paradox

Consider the experience of the insecurely attached child. This child forms two separate internal patterns based on attachment experience. One is a modification of the original attachment behavior. This says that mother is not responding so I must try harder. The child makes an ever-greater effort to modify, enhance, or amplify the attachment behavior in an effort to get mother's attention. The other internal pattern is one that is built on the reaction to unmet needs and leads to fear and, developmentally later, shame. An infant who experiences unmet needs will express frustration and rage. These reactive patterns generalize, as the child grows older and develop full-blown personalities in and of themselves as shall be seen in later chapters.

This concept of generalization is key to understanding brain function. Learning and adaptation cause the brain to become more complex. In other words, we learn to understand the world more simply and easily because the neural nets in our brains become dramatically more complex and interconnected. Michael Hutchison, author of *Mega-Brain*, says, "Stimulation causes structural change in the brain. The brain responds to challenge by becoming more complex, by developing more communication between individual neurons."

Looked at another way threats to the infant's security trigger proximity seeking for the caregiver. When attachment behaviors do not lead to proximity, a new threat emerges, the loss of a necessary relationship. This trigger's further efforts at gaining the proximity of the caregiver, but at the same time, the caregiver's lack of response signals the end of proximity seeking since the behavior is not producing the goal of proximity.

The child is helpless to stop its innate desire to seek proximity through attachment or attention getting behavior. At the same time, however, this attention getting behavior is not going to succeed. This is a paradox. The child has no alternative but to try harder but is motivated to give up at the same time! Paradox sets up complex structures in the brain. Nevertheless, the child cannot give up since the drive toward attachment is so primal. This circular contradiction produces feelings of powerlessness, helplessness, and victimization. To one extent or another, every child, even the securely attached, experiences this paradox.

Attachment as a Continuum

One can imagine the insecure infant constantly believing they will perish through having their security threatened repeatedly. What about this same person as an adult? Some might assume the person would grow out of this. Although the insecurely attached grow up to be rational adults, nothing could be further from the truth! But before talking about adults, I want to say a few words about older children and adolescents.

There is an implicit assumption on the part of some writers in developmental psychology that once attachment is over, it's over. By this, I mean that in child development they study "the attachment phase" as if it ended at some defined point. The problem is not quite so simple. Attachment styles are difficult to change once established. The brain's neural pre-disposition that is built about self-in-relationship is more inflexible when formed under conditions of strain. This is especially true with respect to trauma. Research has shown that the repeated experience of stress and trauma makes neural pathways stronger. Trauma leaves deep permanent etchings in our brain. Nevertheless, the process of attachment is an ongoing one throughout life. We continuously encounter thousands of interactions that become associated with those early preexisting patterns. Each encounter builds upon, modifies, and enhances the last. Remember that the brain is extremely malleable for many years. In addition, it appears that it goes through a major reorganization about every two years.

This gives one hope that the early damage can be undone. It can be. However, the sad truth is those conditions that caused the insecure attachment to begin will often continue, albeit in a modified form, throughout childhood and adolescence. Research indicates that mothers continue the cycle by passing on their own insecure attachment to their children. Therefore, there is a transgenerational aspect giving the process an even greater momentum. I have many female clients, for example, who are in violent relationships, and whose mothers and grandmother were also in violent relationships.

The same patterns of relating that start in infancy continue. If you had an emotionally distant and dismissing mother as a baby, she was probably just as cold and dismissing when you were five years old and when you were ten years old. You are born into a family system. The system will force you to adapt to its unspoken rules, myths, and rituals. This system of interdependent relationships does not suddenly change after the first three years. If anything, it becomes more invasive and oppressive. The basic attachment style is modified and becomes more sophisticated, but no less dramatic and in some cases traumatic. Whatever attachment tendencies are represented in the family system will continue to be reinforced even into adulthood.

For a child, attachment behavior is meant to insure the caregiver's proximity. As adults, we still have an attachment style. It is an accumulation of our internal representations of our "caregivers" availability. This includes all those who have served as attachment surrogates; husbands, wives, girlfriends, boyfriend's - anyone with whom we have formed an intimate relationship. We then judge our ability to use our attachment behaviors to get the closeness we are looking for from our current attachment surrogate.

Amy and Dick, the couple we met above, are playing out their unmet attachment needs on each other. We don't know at this point whether Amy or Dick is securely or insecurely attached. We can see, however, that Amy is seeking unmet needs of approval and that Dick is seeking unmet needs for safety. What happens in a relationship is that we bring our unmet needs with us. The hidden agenda in all relationships of any importance is to convince our partner to fulfill our unmet emotional needs. Mind you, this all happens below the surface of our awareness.

By the time we are adults, our unmet attachment needs have taken on much more complexity then just merely fear or shame. We now have autobiographical memory, which we didn't have during most of the attachment phase. We can now tell an elaborate story to go along with the many repetitive memories that reinforced our unmet needs and subsequently our attachment style.

With adults, secure attachment is different from insecure attachment only by having a higher threshold for activation of attachment behavior. What I mean by this is that when my wife goes to the store, I can tolerate her absence longer if I'm securely attached. I have an internal pattern of self-in-relationship that allows me to soothe any anxieties I may have about her return, at least for a while. At some point, I am going to get agitated. My anxiety will eventually become large enough to override my internal pattern that reassures me. This threshold where anxiety creates internal crisis slides up and down the continuum according to how securely or insecurely attached I am. If I were less securely attached, I might start speculating only five minutes after she had left that she had gone to be with another man. It's this inner felt sense of security that I must access in order to stay stable in a relationship.

I literally am able to go inside and conjure up the necessary self-soothing thoughts and feelings that let me know I am okay. The idea of a threshold makes it far easier to understand the concept of a continuum. Obviously, everyone will have a different trigger point along that continuum. Some may be able to tolerate separation from the attachment figure or surrogate for a few days, others only a few hours, for some just the idea of separation may trigger a state of panic and rage.

If one has an insecure attachment style, the internal picture conjured up may be one of abandonment. The insecurely attached person has no helpful internal representation that aids coping with separation. As adults, the closest intimate relationship becomes a surrogate for the original caregiver, yet one's partner has no power to erase these previous unhealthy patterns of interacting. Each person can only do this for themselves.

Beyond Attachment; the Self-in-Relationship

My work with many angry male patients has shown me that attachment is only one of the ingredients in violent relationships. Counseling is often the last resort when domestic violence becomes an intolerable situation. Sometimes men will come voluntarily and many are forced by the court system. The fear of losing the attachment figure, what is now the wife or girlfriend, is a powerful motivation for a man with insecure attachment.

Nearly all of the relationships I encountered are extremely volatile and explosive. Both partners usually have a personal history that points to insecure attachment. Often, but not always, they have complimentary forms of insecure attachment. For instance, the husband may be avoidant while the wife is fearfully preoccupied. Insecure attachment often results in symptoms of a disorder called the borderline personality. The borderline will be seductive and affectionate one moment and raging the next.

Obviously, people are not all batterers. There has been some interesting research; however, that gives us a glimpse into the continuum of attachment. Donald Dunton in his book, T*he Batterer; a Psychological Profile*, says that it takes three conditions to create a cyclical batterer. The first is insecure attachment to the mother. This damage produces enormous, primitive rage and a paradoxical expectation of disappointment from attachment surrogates throughout life.

The second is shaming from the father. For boys, this often reinforces a sense of worthlessness and a pattern of self-ridicule. The last ingredient in creating a chronic batter is an abusive environment. This abuse can be the ongoing abuse of the child, abuse between parents, and/or a pattern of violence and abuse in the home.

I have heard horrendous stories of abuse from men in domestic violence groups. Sexual abuse is common; including siblings forced to perform for parents. Some have been beaten or humiliated by alcoholic parents. I have heard of beatings with barbed wire, beatings that start when the child is asleep, a sibling forced to beat younger siblings; the range of human degradation has no limits!

In the next chapter, I will show how shame and abuse does not have to be nearly so overt to do lasting damage. Attachment is only the start of the paradox. Once a person is cognitively developed enough to understand the complexities of the world around he, he goes through another phase of adaptation.

Paradoxically, a child learns to be someone they are *not* in order for their real *self* to survive.

Chapter Three

Of Reality, Original Sin, and the Shadow

My wife and I went to a cafe for dinner. In the foyer of the restaurant, there was a large blackboard with the specials of the day printed on it. While my wife walked up closely to inspect the specials, I took a seat in the waiting area.

A she stood there, a small boy walked up behind her. He had been with some adults who were seated in another part of the foyer. As a child will often do, this child walked right up behind her - extremely close, within inches. About then my wife finished reading the board and turned to walk back over toward me. Much to both her and the boy's surprise, she knocked him over like a bowling pin. The boy immediately started to cry. From across the room, an adult male came over to the boy. He bent over and grabbed the boy by one arm pulling him to his feet.

As he did this, he said, "You're okay. You're not hurt." At this point, it was clear the boy was howling not in pain but in shock and fear. Clearly, he had been startled when he was knocked to the floor. My wife apologized to him, and walked over to me. As she did this, I could still hear the man repeating comments that the boy was all right, that he would be okay, and he needn't be upset.

Reality denial starts so soon and so subtly. From the first moments of a child's life, parents and relatives peer into the crib making statements like, "He's a big boy! I wonder what he'll be when he grows up." Our value orientation for boys starts almost at the moment of birth with talk of sports, career choices, and accomplishments. We look into the crib and impart our expectation of some form of heroism. The problem with this is that later in life, it becomes a kind of death sentence. Men find that they are defined not in terms of who they are but in terms of what they do. The message is, "Be a hero." To be a hero is to be a cardboard cut out of a real person, not a human being.

Meanwhile, a little girl lies in her crib listening to cooing and awing about how beautiful she is. "I'll bet she'll be a heart breaker." "She'll be a beauty when she grows up." Too often these are the first strangling seeds planted in a woman's life that transform into the misery of negative self-evaluation, repeated dieting, self criticism, and feelings of body shame. If the family system develops in a certain way, these seeds could lead to anorexia. A little of our junk culture added to the adolescent experience and anorexia becomes a death sentence.

This may seem overly dramatic. But, consider what's really going on at the crib. No one is saying, "I can hardly wait to get to know this new person." "I want to spend time with this person." "I wonder what will be unique about this person." "What can I learn that will be surprising and wonderful from this new life?"

Rather we immediately start imposing our culturally distorted view of reality. The message imbedded in the communication at the crib is, "be who I tell you to be, not who you are." This coded message becomes part of the actual structure of the brain, which as we pointed out earlier, continues to develop in dramatic fashion.

Later, when the child falls and hurts him or herself we say, "There, there, it's all right." We deny their reality, their hurt, and take care of our own anxiety instead. The child knows it is not all right. However, we don't make it okay for them to say, "I'm scared and it hurts."

"You'll be okay. You're not really hurt." We would never think of entering their world. "Come on, shake it off." It's not about their pain anyway. It's all about us. We are busy running from our own pain. We have no tolerance for a child's pain.

Depending on cultural, these massages may be contradictory but no less paradoxical. If we are Anglos we say, "Hey, look at me when I talk to you!" If we are Hispanic we say, "Hey, don't look at me when I talk to you!"

"God damn it! Stop crying or I'll give you something to cry about!"

The coded messages here are, "your experience is not valid. Your feelings are not legitimate. You are not important; I am important." "If you want to know what is real, you must ask me." "Your perception of reality is not real. I will tell you what is real and what is not real." "You're not a legitimate person as long as I'm here. In fact, I have the power to tell you when to be legitimate and when to be invisible." "Don't be. Be only when it reflects favorably on me. Your existence is about my feelings and my needs."

"Are you still here? How inconvenient! This is for your own good."

As you read this you may be protesting, "My mother and father never talked to me that way."

First, much of the actual communication of this devaluing of a child is nonverbal. Much of it is very sweet. "Honey, we Morgensterns never cry. Go wipe your eyes so your father doesn't see you. What a good girl!"

This effort at dehumanization is eventually passed on from the parents to the children. The family forms a system of roles, conventions, and behaviors. The family becomes, as famed British psychiatrist R. D. Laing puts it in his landmark work, *the Politics of the Family*, "a transpersonal system of collusion." - a gooey mess.

The family says non-verbally, "Susie will grow up to be the Doctor. You, however, will be the 'ne'er do well' son of the family. And since Dad is emotionally distant and you're never going anywhere with your life anyway, you are assigned to be Mom's emotional support. She will use you as a surrogate husband, recruit you to join her against him, and incest you emotionally. She will put her need for emotional comfort over your need to be a separate person. Consequently, you will never successfully marry or launch into adulthood. You will stay triangulated with Mom and Dad."

They all conspire unconsciously parceling out the family roles and alliances. Then the family acts to deny the collusion and to operate on reality until they create and believe another version.

You might think that this characterization is harsh. The family has rules, secrets, and agreements. These are imprinted into each child. Then the existence of these rules, secrets, and agreements is denied to complete another step in the paradox.

"I wonder why he just doesn't move out of the house. I couldn't stand to spend every day with Mother. That would drive me nuts."

"Give her a break! How would you like to come home to a thirty-five-year-old son who can't hold a job and who smokes pot and who is financially dependent on you?"

"At least Dad gets some piece of mind. He just mentally checks out and spends all of his time in the basement."

One of my clients came to therapy with a life long problem of being anxious. When stressed, she would get migraines, vomit, and stay in bed most of the time. Her mother had explained this as a child's response to the neighbor's dog barking under the child's window. "You were frightened of the dog, dear." Actually, my patient spent her childhood sharing a bed with her sister who was being molested by their father. Possibly, Dad heard the dog barking too. I wonder if it frightened him

As we shall establish later, the part of the child that hates what is happening is split off into the world of the shadow. There are also other parts of us that feel frightened and guilty because of our hatred and anger hidden in the shadow of the psyche. And even hatred for the abuser gets invalidated since, as we just saw, the abuse itself is often denied. Thus, we learn to hate the part that hates. Invalidated feelings must go somewhere. We will see that the shadow is a good place for them.

As stated above, in order to adopt the family's version of reality we must disavow our experience. Of course, our private disavowal goes hand-in-hand with the role of the family in paradoxically excommunicating our experience.

Many clients come in to my office and say that their childhood was normal. I can see one person in my mind right now, a distinguished looking man in his early '60s. After a few sessions, he finally admitted that his Dad hit him and broke his nose when he was four years old. That was the first time. During a pause in the conversation, he would compulsively count ceiling tiles or any other geometric shapes in the room.

Adoptive parents had raised another client. As a teenager, she had developed a skin condition. Instead of seeking treatment, her parents constantly reminded her of how ugly it looked, concluding that she would probably never attract a man. She had "forgotten" most of this by the time she came to see me.

The point behind all of this is that we must tailor our perception of our own experience, even our memories, in order to avoid serious trouble with a society that is in total denial. Early in our lives, it might be considered cute to say that the Emperor has no clothes. However, in order to grow up and be good members of our family and our world, we must learn to repress our perception and our legitimate experience. We learn to literally see what they see, hear what they hear. We distort our perception. In so doing we deny ourselves. We seal off our real selves and replace them with those *parts* that have learned to adapt and survive the abuse of "true self" denial.

R. D. Laing, the British psychiatrist, put it this way: "our family of origin has done its best. It has given us a range of distinctions, options, identities, definitions, rules, repertories of operations, instructions, attributions, loci, scenarios, roles, parts to play . . . But it has not told us who are "we" who play those parts and take up those positions"

Value judgments from parents, teachers, and other authorities force us to replace our real selves with a cartoon character that pleases the world. Laing goes on:

> "We like their food served up elegantly before us: we do not want to know about the animal factories, the slaughterhouses, and what goes on in the kitchen. Our own cities are our own animal factories; families, schools, churches are the real slaughterhouses of our children; colleges and other places are the kitchens. As adults in marriage and business, we eat the product."

However, be assured. The principles outlined in this book shine a bright light along the path that leads away from this grim scene to a life of freedom. Freedom to pick the reality that gives us true power and inner peace.

Freud's Naked Emperor

The father of psychology fell in to the trap we have been discussing. Freud learned the lesson of accepting the collective reality almost at his peril. While his contribution to the social science of psychology was staggering, it could have been even greater had he not been driven to deny himself and his clients, in order to make his version of reality more palatable to his colleagues.

Freud originally set out to find the cause of "hysteria" in his population of women patients. And he did. What he discovered as a cause was incest and sexual abuse. The cause of "hysteria" would not surprise us today. Today, no doubt, we would diagnose these women as having posttraumatic stress disorder or PTSD. PTSD gained notoriety when Vietnam veterans came home with symptoms that included flash backs and night terrors.

Nevertheless, Freud's findings were widely criticized as being unacceptable to the medical community of his day. This put Freud in a horrible dilemma. If he stuck to his findings, he would probably never have achieved the acclaim that he ultimately earned. Stung by the criticism of his theory that childhood incest and sexual abuse caused adult female hysteria, he went back to the drawing board to find a theory that was more acceptable. Unfortunately, the reality of the women who needed help was sacrificed in the process. It was much easier for the medical community of Freud's day to accept that boys were frightened of castration and girls subconsciously wanted a penis than to face the fact that adults, themselves, could be so misguided and filled with pain as to violate young children.

It's ironic that this paradox is embedded in the birth of psychology is. Freud illustrated what happens to our perception of reality when it clashes with the greater, more general view of society. It is one thing physically or sexually to abuse a child. But denying the child's experience, a child's worldview no matter how small, and their legitimate rights to be separate, special people, is a form of abuse. It rewires the brain and stays with each of us for the rest of our lives. In the absence of overt abuse, we all still experience a more subtle form. If we don't beat them or violate them, we undermine their right to be who they really are and thrust them into paradox.

We must not make light of the outrageous and epidemic level of abuse reported to various types of government authorities. The U.S. Department of Health and Human Services reports that 1,012,000 children were victims of substantiated abuse in 48 states in 1994. 53% suffered neglect, 26 percent physical abuse, 14 percent sexual abuse, 5 percent emotional abuse, and 22 percent some other form of maltreatment. In that same year, 1,111 children died because of abuse. From 1989 to 1994, 5,400 children were killed in 43 states through acts of abuse.

A new study just released says that one in seven women was sexually abused as children. This same study revealed that one in three men reported being physically abused as children. In addition, one in ten of all those surveyed said that they had been severely abused physically including scalding, choking, and punching. That's a lot of angry, emotionally damaged people.

Original Sin

I believe the traditional story of the Garden of Eden foretold these same principles, which we have been discussing. This story holds the key to the lowest common denominator and explains, in a religious context, our dilemma as humans.

In the traditional story of the Garden of Eden, we know that God allowed Adam and Eve free reign to explore and partake of the Garden. Genesis reads, "Every tree was pleasant to the site and good for food." In addition, it points out two trees in particular: the Tree of Life and the Tree of the Knowledge of Good and Evil. God says to Adam that he is forbidden to eat the fruit of the Tree of the Knowledge of Good in Evil, for "the day that he does he will surely die."

Notice that God is not saying they cannot eat from the Tree of Life. Presumably, Adam and Eve can eat all they want of the fruit of the Tree of Life. In fact, having Abundant Life, Life Everlasting, and Eternal Life are recurrent themes throughout the Old and New Testament. We will lift these concepts out of their religious frame of reference and deal with them in a later chapter.

For now, it is important to see that God is giving Adam the choice between life and death. It's just that simple. What is it about the knowledge of "good" and "evil" that is so deadly? Knowing "good" and "evil," according to the Serpent, is like being a god. What would be wrong with that?

In *Owning Your Own Shadow* by Robert Johnson, the shadow is labeled as the dark side of the psyche. Of our shadow he says, "This is our legacy from having eaten of the fruit of the Tree of Knowledge in the Garden of Eden." Johnson is saying that the shadow *parts* in humankind are a result of "original sin." More on the shadow in a few moments. But just what is this knowledge we supposedly partook of all about? What is it about knowing "good" and "evil" that does damage to the point of "death" in humankind and creates the Shadow in the process?

When the author of Genesis, presumably Moses, used the terms "good" and "evil" what was he trying to say? It may seem simple until you read other translations in addition to the King James Version. The Jerusalem Bible does not translate the same passage using the words "good" and "evil." Instead, it uses the words "blessing" and "misfortune."

In Rotherham's Emphasized Bible, the notes to the same passage give the words "blessing" and "misfortune" as an alternative. The Amplified Bible goes even a step further. It translates the passage as "good and evil and blessing and calamity."

What is there about blessing and misfortune or calamity that is not conveyed with the words "good an evil?" Good and evil are like black and white, top and bottom, inside and outside, up or down. The words "blessing and misfortune" have a different quality of meaning. There has to be a personal interpretation of the meaning. Someone has to say this is a "blessing" and this is a "misfortune." The concepts of "blessing and misfortune" need an interpreter. Is a "blessing" still a blessing even if no one notices it? I don't know, but we are much less likely to ask that question of "good." Good is good. Does our approval make good more or less likely? No. There is some apparent inner knowingness about good. Nevertheless, there has to be an observer in order to determine the quality of experience as a "blessing" or a "misfortune."

Oddly enough, we know that often times a "blessing" can be a "misfortune." In addition, sometimes what appears to be a "misfortune" turns out to be a "blessing in disguise." How do we make the distinction then? It seems clear to me that in order to determine what is a blessing and what is a misfortune; we must make a value judgment. I am not referring here to ethics, principles, ideals, standards, or morals. Those are *values*.

A "value" judgment, on the other hand, is the act of assessing the worth or merit of the situation, a person, or any thing. However, what if our "value" judgments are wrong? What if we suddenly, being like a god, judge, blame, and find fault without the benefit of the God-like qualities of omniscience and omnipotence?

So what? We do it anyway. We take it upon ourselves automatically to judge each situation as a "blessing" or a "misfortune." We have developed a keen sense for value judging. Often we can do it without even being present at an event or knowing the facts. Each of us in our own way becomes a "value judge."

Then we teach our children to do it through our example. They, of course, will teach their children to do it through their example. This act of preparing each succeeding generation to make the inevitable value judgments of life sows the seeds of death and re-enacts original sin. As the serpent predicted, we become like gods all right. We arrogantly enter each situation with our pre-conceptions and our notions of good and evil. We label, we evaluate, and we judge, and in so doing we shut off the flow of life thereby refusing to see all other possibilities. Our insistence on being right, being in control, making our point, and assuming we know the value or lack thereof of each instant of life strangles the life force that lives within us, forcing it down out of sight.

We insist that we know what is okay and what is not okay, what is acceptable and what is not. We make value judgments always and everywhere. Every move we make is tainted with value judgments. Then we pass this ability on to our children as parents and as a culture in subtle and not so subtle forms of abuse. How? We presume to judge our children. We "tell" them what part of them is good and what part is evil.

Remember what happened to Adam and Eve. After they had eaten the forbidden fruit of the knowledge of good in evil, they suddenly realized that they were naked and covered themselves because they were ashamed. If you read the text, you'll notice that they are not ashamed because of what they have done. Now that they have the ability to make a value judgment about themselves, *they are ashamed of who they are.* They cover up and try to hide from God. It is a funny thing about value judgments. Adam and Eve are suddenly aware that they are naked and now have the capacity of feeling shame.

The psychology of shame is about identity and personhood, not just a feeling of embarrassment. In his book, *The Batterer: a Psychological Profile,* Donald Dutton says, "Shame is a response to an attack on the global sense of self. When we are shamed, our very sense of who we are is threatened."

Shaming is an attack on one's right to be alive. Shame is a feeling of having no worth as a person, of being in disgrace. Shame is the "fruit" of the knowledge of good and evil.

Our seemingly innate ability to make value judgments about our world and its people is a death sentence. God tells Adam and Eve about the results of their action - grief, suffering, desire, craving, sorrow, toil, sweat and finally back to dust. That was one bad apple!

This is commonly interpreted as punishment from God for man's disobedience. Is this true? Or is this the "fruit" of the Tree of the Knowledge of Blessing and Misfortune? Through the lens of value judgments, life takes on characteristics of striving, lack, and want. The transgenerational process of original sin blocks peace and abundant life. How can we find peace when we're constantly evaluating and interpreting?

As the little boy picked himself up from the floor at the restaurant where my wife had accidentally knocked him over, I wondered if he was consciously aware that he had been shamed by that adult who insisted on denying the child's reality and ignoring his fear and pain.

Robert Johnson says of this process, "Culture takes away the simple human in us, but gives us a more complex and sophisticated power."

Creating the Shadow

Jeff remembers what happened like it was yesterday. He sits in the chair opposite me and closes his eyes occasionally as if to get a better look at the interior landscape.

He was two years old. It was evening. Jeff stood near the fireplace in the living room of the family home. He describes his clothing as one of those pajama outfits with the feet attached to the legs. He can see his father and sister sitting at the dining room table. His father is raging at his sister.

The screaming and verbal abuse goes on in an all too familiar pattern for what seems to be an eternity. I notice that Jeff appears visibly shaken as he recounts the details. Finally, he looks up at me with tears in his eyes. I can see terror and grief mixed in with the tears.

"That's when I made the decision."

"Go on," I urge him.

"I decided that what was happening to my sister was not going to happen to me - couldn't happened to me. That's when I decided I had to be perfect. I had to become perfect so that would never happen to me."

"So, there's a part of you that needs to look perfect to keep you safe?"

"Right."

"What about the fear you felt?"

"Oh, I could never show him fear. I just concentrated on doing the right thing so he wouldn't hurt me."

The human shadow is a metaphor for those parts of us that we do not want to see, or that would not be safe to show to others. Like Jeff's fear, one won't let it into the light. In fact, the more light one shines on one's self, the clearer and more sharply defined is one's the shadow. When we are very young, a light is directly above us, but as the years pass, the shadow we cast can be long indeed.

The poet Robert Bly, in *A Little Book on the Human Shadow*, likens the process to a very long bag that we drag behind us. Parents, teachers, and society in general tell us which of our qualities are acceptable and which are unacceptable.

As has been stated, the attachment process sets a tone that is generalized into our sense of self-in-relationship. Attachment is the beginning of how we internally represent ourselves in relationship to others. Part of this generalization is a child's response to negative evaluations from his or her primary caregivers. At 3 to 5 years of age, a child will interpret repeated value judgments from parents as meaning there is something wrong with him or her, with his or her quality of being in the world. This is a direct threat to security, and self-existence. An infant will do any thing to survive. That includes emotionally cutting off a part of themselves and banishing it forever to the shadow self, the parts they don't want to look at.

This can be seen with the avoidant child in the "strange situation" in the previous chapter. He or she has learned to override the innate drive toward proximity with the caregiver. In so doing, he or she denies an essential part of himself or herself.

As the child gets older, the child automatically disowns his or her parts in order to become more acceptable to parents. Just as Jeff disowns his fear and splits off a part of him that was supposed to be perfect, we soon learn to automate the process of splitting, fracturing, and fragmenting our Limbic system. In the process, we lose our true selves and our sense of unity with the world. This is the effect of Original Sin. Splitting means spiritual isolation.

An active child may be taught that he or she is "bad" when behaving wildly. The child soon learns what part must be hidden in order to remain safe and secure. Children of alcoholics learned early to put their anger into Bly's "bag" since anger at the alcoholic's erratic behavior can provoke a life threatening response.

Bly says, "By the time my brother and I were 12 . . . we were known as 'the nice Bly boys.' Our bags were nearly a mile long." This paints a powerful and pitiful picture of what it takes to make sure adults see only those parts of us that are pleasing to them.

The effects of original sin are complete. We have learned from our first moments just like Adam and Eve that we are naked and we should hide from God (our parents). We are to feel ashamed of ourselves while not believing what we think or perceive as legitimate reality.

Chapter Four

Multiplicity

In his book, *Fuzzy Thinking*, Bart Kosko refers to a concept he calls a "pattern of activation" as a basic process of the brain. He also refers to brain patterns as holographic, which is an idea we will come back to later. This "pattern of activation" is a function of the basic thinking/learning structure of the brain - neural networks. Neural networks are interconnections that set up a pattern of activation. What this means is that neural networks have a habitual inclination or tendency to be activated in a certain way over and over again.

This concept plays out dramatically in my house everyday. One of our two cats, SC (sweet cat) has a pattern of activation organized around the idea of tuna. His neural networks have a habitual tendency to think of the world in terms of tuna. Everything that happens in the kitchen is first and foremost about tuna. If the refrigerator door opens, it's about tuna. If I walk into the kitchen, it's about tuna. SC spends his waking life *scanning* for tuna. Occasionally his habitual tendency turns out to be right. Then his entire brain resonates with tuna.

Antonio Damasio, who wrote *Descartes' Error*, calls this idea a "dispositional representation." The dispositional representation is a habitual inclination that causes input to the brain to stand for or symbolize a pattern that is already there. For SC, each new experience with tuna builds upon, as well as modifies, the existing neural networks that hold the pattern of activation for tuna.

Neural nets self-organize and converge. Bart Kosko likens it to a ball rolling down a well and coming to a stop. Concepts like habitual inclination, pattern of activation, and dispositional representation give us the idea that the brain is a little fuzzy. Neural nets are skewed towards a tendency. They have a habit of converging in a certain way until they learned otherwise. Kosko says, "...a *thought* is an energy well or point of resonance. *Thinking* is the ball falling into the well, the road to resonance . . . We can also dig a well at the center or average of many experiences. The new experiences are old and 'real' but the average is new . . . We generalized as our neural nets dig wells . . ."

For our cat, SC, an entire wall of neurons vibrate or resonate with incoming data that, in a fuzzy way, matches the pattern of his association for tuna. This could be the smell of tuna, a noise associated with tuna like the can opener, the look of tuna, the taste or texture of tuna, or even the memory of tuna. Then, just like the pull of gravity, the patterns converge and are activated just like a ball falling into a well. Curiously, the ball (or thought) that falls in to the well of the neural net changes the net itself with the quality of that experience. The network takes that experience into account the next time a ball falls in the well of pattern recognition buy rewiring itself. Thus, the neural network lies in the brain waiting for the next pattern to activate its habitual tendency in much, but never the *exact* way that it had been activated before.

Attachment as well as all of our early learning experiences organized themselves in the Limbic System as described above. Of course, each piece of experience has any number of neural nets that make up patterns of association and habitual tendencies. Add all these together and you have a complete way of being or self-in-relationship associated with the most common experiences we have.

Our attachment style is the sum of all of the neural nets that make up the patterns that give us our habitual tendencies in relationships. If the "well" represents "relationships" then attachment is at the bottom of the well. However, as we have shown in the last chapter, we organize these experiences and memories in segments according to our previous lessons on survival in a world filled with judgment.

But before we go further with this idea, let's play a little guessing game. I'm thinking of a fruit, that is round and brightly colored and is sour when I bite into it.

A habitual tendency inside your brain would have *scanned* those words and synchronized with the description. At the point of synchronization, an image of a lemon or some other fruit would have popped into your mind. It may have included sounds, probably taste, and many other images including memories. This response to the synchronization of input with the pattern of activation is *enormous* and is spread out all over the brain's topology. This process involves countless neural networks forming patterns of activation and dispositional representations all over the brain and includes many, if not most, of the processing regions of the brain. The brain operates using dozens and dozens of parallel processors.

Given this foundation of understanding, we can now make a logical leap from a lemon to a relationship. Attachment styles, self-preserving strategies, and patterns of self-in-relationship are all wired into the Limbic System. Our experience of a lemon would also be wired into limbic structures if we had been forced to eat them repeatedly without sugar during our early stages of development.

The Parts of a "Borderline"

Thinking about the Limbic System organized around habitual tendencies and patterns of activation, it's not a huge leap to see how the brain could organize and generalize all of these into a complex neural structure that includes perception, activation, and behavior. This gives us the possibility that the brain forms many personalities.

Therefore, it is my contention that the Limbic System forms itself into sub-personalities or what are often called *parts*. The term "parts" is widely used in a casual sense to differentiate between various internal experiences. We're all familiar with someone who says to us, "a *part* of me wants to do this, but another *part* of me wants to do that."

Psychiatrists and psychologists know that the brain can organize itself into *parts*. When this happens and causes mental illness, it is termed multiple personality disorder, MPD. Recently the name for this disorder has been changed to Dissociative Identity Disorder, DID. We all have learned to associate MPD with different distinct parts of a person. What causes MPD? Research has proven that MPD is caused by extreme child abuse. There are countless documented cases of the unimaginable abuse it takes to give birth to MPD. One in particular case stands out in my mind. A small boy's grandfather often buried him alive with only a pipe for a breathing tube. If that weren't torture enough, the grandfather would then urinate down the tube. In order to deal with a situation so extreme, the brain has to disassociate by splitting off *parts* that deal with the experience and *parts* that have no memory of it.

The ability of the brain to create personalities on the fly to deal with trauma, chronic terror, and/or extreme abuse tells us that we have an innate ability to organize the Limbic System into sub-personalities. Just as attachment experiences exist along a continuum, the brain's effort at coping by creating sub-personalities occurs along a continuum as well. At one end of the continuum are "normal people." At the other end of the continuum are those with MPD. What is interesting about this is when psychology students go through graduate school and learn about psychosis and personality disorders they begin to feel like they have all of them. In a way we all do, since we're all somewhere along the continuum of creating sub-personalities in the Limbic System in order to survive our early experience.

Another mental disorder that highlights this process in a way that is easy to see is called the Borderline Personality. I am using Borderline Personality Disorder as an example because it highlights dramatically the principles of internal *parts* formation in an external way. The term "borderline" was adopted because these people could be seen as having features of both neurosis and psychosis and were on the borderline between the two. To put it in psychological vernacular, the borderline has *neurotic* fears of *abandonment* on the one hand, and *psychotic rage* on the other.

Meet Beth and Jim. Beth is a young homemaker with an infant daughter. Her husband, Jim, is an attorney. They are in their early 30s, an attractive couple, and to all appearances, they have everything going for them. Nothing could be further from the truth.

If you listen to his story, he will tell you of a wife who rages at him, constantly threatens to leave, continually refers to old boyfriend's, and who threatens to withhold sex for a variety of reasons. If you listened her story, she will tell you about husband who physically attacks her, withholds money and other family resources, and who attempts to keep her a prisoner in her own home which keeps her from buying food for their infant..

Despite this stormy relationship, the couple does go through brief periods of sublime happiness and marital bliss. This often leads to passionate sex that results afterwards in one of the two of them flying into a jealous rage, and the cycle continues.

What is surprising is how different they present themselves in therapy despite the fact that they both have all of the major features of a Borderline Personality Disorder. Beth presents as the stricken victim of a batterer. Jim presents as a sophisticated and intelligent professional who has his act together, but is saddled with a "hysterical" wife.

I have worked with many borderline men. Nearly all batterers have features of Borderline Personality Disorder. The fear of abandonment always stems from insecure attachment. The rage is also primal and results from a feeling of helplessness and a desperate attempt to exert control over, as well as punish the attachment figure. This is nothing more than an extension of the attachment "control" system where the infant is trying to control the proximity of the caregiver. Of course, it is not uncommon for these men to have been severely mistreated as children.

Men typically deny their rage and abusive behavior, and come across as reasonable although perhaps manipulative. Their fear of abandonment is rarely displayed in the therapy room or in men's groups. This makes total sense since men in our culture are physically or emotionally punished for showing any feelings of sensitivity or vulnerability almost from the moment they can crawl. Nevertheless, in a relationship with an attachment surrogate like a wife, it comes out as jealousy, controlling behavior, and begging for reconciliation after a fight or outburst of violence. Men have long evaded the appropriate "borderline" diagnosis since they "act" so differently in therapy than they do in intimate relationships. Men do this due to their fear of humiliation and shame when it comes to the display of emotions other than anger.

Women with borderline features are far different from men in a therapeutic setting since the therapist becomes an attachment surrogate. Men don't normally allow this to happen in therapy. Also, women are not generally socialized to hate their emotions, and so permission to display them is implied in the therapeutic relationship. No one type of client stirs up more "counter transference" in the therapist than a borderline. Counter-transference is a psychological term that refers to the feelings that get stirred up in the therapist when working with the client, as opposed to "transference," which are feelings that the client has toward the therapist. A therapist must be on guard and monitoring their emotional reactivity at all times when working with a borderline. If a male therapist is not careful, he will have protective and possibly even sexual feelings for his female client. Borderline women may try to recruit the therapist to be close, overly close. It is difficult to keep a professional distance unless the therapist realizes this is a "borderline" and has a therapeutic map in place for guidance.

Just about the time the therapist (male or female) has a good rapport with the client, she will attack! She will attack in whatever way will hurt the most: competence, compassion, or intelligence. Female borderlines seem to sense a therapist's vulnerabilities and they will go straight for them. This is what they do in all of their intimate relationships. The gender of the therapist makes no difference. The temptation to attack back and defend is powerful for the therapist. Soon the therapist may be fighting off feelings of hatred. The therapist wants this client out of his or her life forever! He or she wonders where all of these feelings coming from.

Suddenly the female borderline will shift away from rage and start begging the therapist not to abandon her by being seductive. In my early days is a therapist, I always knew when I had been with a woman client who had borderline tendencies. Afterward I would be filled with contradictory feelings of hatred and attraction. It was frightening. I would never know whether she would cling or rage. I would come into each session half-sick to my stomach, ready to set new rules and establish boundaries only to have my plans sabotaged by manipulation and counter attack.

A friend of mind, a female therapist, described her first experience with a borderline in many of the same terms. Her client finally fired her as her therapist just like the female borderline had fired the six therapists before. Moreover, the patient told my friend that she never thought my friend was qualified to do her any good. The patient said my friend was not professional in her conduct. My friend was exasperated and devastated. Without an anchor and a plan, this kind of experience can be disorienting and unnerving for a therapist.

Once a therapist knows what they're dealing with, borderlines can be helped successfully. However, the first experience with one leaves you wondering if this is really the right profession. Many mature professionals simply will not work with a "borderline" because it can be so hard on the therapist.

I am reminded of a woman client who has borderline tendencies. She starts each session complaining that her husband won't spend enough time with her, just uses her, and won't get close. Then she complains that he wants to be too close to her and that she's not ready. She will often sob, and through her tears accuse him of not loving her, on the one hand, and in the same sentence tell him that she wants him to stay away from her - she wants nothing more to do with him. This "I love you/I hate you" seesaw, this "come closer-further way" battle, is typical of people with borderline tendencies.

All this being said, I want to qualify the term "borderline." I believe that this classification of personality disorder is commonly misapplied. Thanks to the pioneering work of Judith Herman and her book, *Trauma and Recovery*, we now know that borderline features are more likely the result of Post-Traumatic Stress Disorder. In fact, Herman proposes a new classification called Complex Post-Traumatic Stress Disorder.

Borderline personality characteristics are the result of abuse and insecure attachment. As with Freud and "hysteria," the borderline diagnosis is yet another, albeit unintentional, refusal of the mental health establishment to confront the abuse of women. The same applies to men. Although Herman's book deals with abuse from a feminist's perspective, the plight of men is no less misunderstood. All of the men I have seen that are batterers were abused extensively as children. Boys are more often beaten, tormented, and publicly humiliated while girls are most often molested, treated as if they are incompetent, and disempowered. However, the long-term symptoms are more accurately the result of Post-Traumatic Stress Syndrome and not a personality disorder.

The Two Faces of the Borderline

From the above discussion, it appears that the therapist may be dealing with two people instead of one. There is one person who craves closeness and will beguile, seduce, and even pretend to make therapeutic progress to get the reward of being close. Then there is the other person who emerges as an attacking, punitive warrior. These two behaviors seemed to be at opposite extremes. What's going on? Their relationships at home are no less explosive.

Dr. James Masterson has done much pioneering work in the theory and treatment of both borderline and narcissistic personality disorders. He calls the process that creates a borderline a splitting defense mechanism in early childhood. He claims the child splits him or herself into two parts, a good self and a bad self, neither of which are the real self. This is the adaptation of the Limbic System. This split that results in borderline features is the result of ambivalent attachment where the baby seeks contact with the primary caregiver but pushes away angrily as was discussed earlier. What this produces is two distinct personalities or patterns of how to be in the world that are linked to one another. Just like the ambivalent attachment, the borderline has two *parts* in the same sort of conflict.

This is a person locked in the paradox of needing closeness, but also who knows, because their caregiver did not respond appropriately, that the behavior designed to produce closeness will fail. The result is rage. In the borderline, this process is more generalized since it applies not just to the primary caregiver but also to attachment surrogates like boyfriends, girlfriends, husbands, wives, and so forth. It is also more complex since coupled with rage are more complex rationalizations and speculations that lead to jealousy, insecurity, and controlling behavior. As the brain has become more developed, their worldview has adapted to a more complex world and they have developed an autobiographical story of self-in-relationship.

What's really going on here are two distinct personalities at work within the borderline, one who desperately wants closeness and one who wants to punish attachment surrogates for their predictable lack of response of the original caregiver. The person is shifting back and forth between two of their own internal *parts* that are polarized against one another, locked into a paradox of need and disappointment.

There is a growing body of evidence that the brain's organization is modular, made up of many parallel processors that work independently of one another, which converge to create perception and meaning and to initiate behavior. Each scans for its own version of reality, ready to activate an entire system of responses that are discrete from other modules. These modules can be entire sub-personalities.

I have chosen the example of a Borderline Personality Disorder for two reasons. First, there is an uncanny resemblance between ambivalent attachment and the behavior style of a borderline - clinging and pushing away. Secondly, it is one of the easiest ways to see *multiplicity* at work. There are two distinct *parts* or sub-personalities that clearly standout; the *part* of them that frantically seeks closeness, and the *part* that defends against the pain of closeness through rage.

Pain and defense against pain are internal splits that all of us have to one degree or another. We shall see how these *parts* of us work more clearly later. Instead of borderline, I could have chosen Disassociative Identity Disorder (formerly Multiple Personality Disorder) since we have all learned to associate MPD with different distinct *parts* of the person. I could have even used the

Avoidant Personality Disorder where one *part* wants contact with people and the other *part* is afraid of shame and ridicule, and therefore, keeps away from social contact.

In fact, I believe all of the personality disorders can be explained through attachment and subsequent abuse, and family System pressures that result in a variety of different splits between shame or fear and defenses against those feelings. In the case of someone with borderline features, the splitting between two *parts* is easy to observe and understand in the context of attachment and the internal organization of self-in-relationship. It makes a good example to start with.

The Modular Brain

Before going on, let's review a few of the things we've said about the brain. First, the brain consists of three different structures. Brain scientist, Paul McClain, called this the *triune brain* theory. The Reptilian Brain or R-Complex includes the lower in mid-brain areas of the spinal cord. It keeps us alive physiologically, let's us move about, and is the source of instincts, primitive sensations, aggression, and reproduction, to name a few.

The Limbic System, or Mammalian Brain, is the seat of emotions, conditioning, memory, hormones, complex sensations, and perceptions. The Neo-Cortex (Cerebral Cortex) the newest part of brain, lays on top of the rest of the brain and gives us our language abilities, vision, perceptual learning, hearing - all of the things that make us distinctly human. The Frontal Lobes of the Neo-Cortex give us are social maps of how to be in the world as social animals. In this part of the brain, we have our adult ideas of self-in-relation ship when we are not emotionally reactive.

The Neo-Cortex distinguishes man. Other mammals have no Neo-Cortex. All creatures except man have their brains nearly fully development at birth. In man, the Neo-Cortex represents eighty-five percent of brain mass, and it is not fully developed at birth. Pelvis size does not match head size in humans; therefore, most of higher order brain development must occur in the years after birth, after the head passes through the pelvis. Remember the Garden of Eden? God told Adam and Eve that, after the "fall of man." childbearing would be painful. Once we have passed through the birth canal, our heads can get bigger. The last part of the brain to develop is the thinking cap of the frontal lobes. This means that the Limbic System acquires our emotionally driven behaviors long before the adult brain has much to say about it!

While we may have this wonderful social computer upstairs, by the time we learn to use it, we are already an "emotional basket case." Our reactions to self-in-relationship are highly conditioned toward unproductive behaviors, poor choices, anxiety, fear, and aggression. This is due to early learning about what *part* of us is okay and not okay, and how to survive the Family System and our junk culture.

Descartes postulated that inside the brain was a *homunculus*, a Chairman of the Board, or general manager who sat at a big set of controls, kind of like the Wizard of OZ. Everything in the brain ran through him or her for clearance and approval. At the very least, there must be a center of convergence or a neurological central node of some kind. The modern day metaphor for this would be the *Transformer* - a mighty robot with the hero inside the head manipulating the controls.

Richard Restak points out in his book, *The Modular Brain*, that modern brain researchers "have debunked this idea of some central point of command . . . all brain cells and collections of brain cells communicate with other cells. This means that no "pontifical" cell or area holds sway over all others, nor do all areas in the brain 'report' to an overall supervisory center."

Our experience of self-in-relationship to the world is not the result of one central perception. The brain organizes perception in a modular fashion, distributed over many areas of the networks of neurons, many modules operating in parallel fashion. This may seem disconcerting at first. Where is the soul? Where is the seat of consciousness? Where is *me*?

Antonio Damasio in his groundbreaking work on emotion, reason, and the human brain, *Descartes' Error*, states that consciousness is something that arises out of the brain-body ensemble. Or as George Page said in the PBS series, *The Brain*, "The mind is what the brain does." Damasio defines consciousness as the "self perturbed." Our awareness or consciousness is a result of comparing one state of being with another. In order to change our state, something must have changed or perturbed us. The use of the term "self perturbed" designates change rather than a positive or negative state of being.

When We "Feel" an Emotion

As we discussed earlier, the cornerstone of brain function can be described with various phrases like habitual tendency, pattern of association, or dispositional representation, which is Damasio's term. As we perceive new data, internal representations are fired in neurons that once held patterns that may or may not be somewhat similar to the new data. Damasio suspects that when a certain synchronization of the externally generated perception with the internally replicated pattern happens a "topographically organized representation" is activated. Like a ball falling in a well, the neural nets converge. He calls it "topographical" because it is literally spread out all over the brain. While this may or may not be an accurate replication of the earlier firing pattern held in the neural connections, these topographically organized patterns lead to the recall of images that form memories.

The mechanisms that trigger these recalled images or memories are those patterns of association. They are groups of neurons that form convergence zones with the potential to fire in a particular pattern. They hold within their relationship the ability to recreate any image. They appear to be located all over the higher order association cortex. When fired, they activate the sensory parts of the brain creating an image. Many of these habitual tendencies or patterns of association would need to fire to recall the face of a friend or to hear her voice, for example. Like Restak, Damasio says these patterns of association fire image and sensory patterns, i.e. topographically organized patterns, scattered all over the brain. So, there is no single residing place for our friend in memory. The potential to recreate the experience of her is widely distributed. This process of dispositional representation is elastic and subject to error. It would have to be elastic or we would not recognize our own face in the mirror, as we grew older.

Imagine the experience of looking at our friend. As we look at our friend, we consciously consider our relationship with her. The brain undergoes a process that involves the creation of both verbal and nonverbal representations of words, sentences, a likeness of her, or places were she has been seen. This pattern of processing occurs under the guidance of habitual tendencies that are firing a series of topographical representations that activate the sensory, auditory, and visual parts of the brain. It is almost as if our patterns of association were like ushers in a dark theater. They lead us down the aisles shining a light along each row. If there is a "fit," a row of empty seats, our mind is flooded with remembered images in the form of these topographically organized firing patterns. Therefore, we think "Oh! Here is a place to sit down."

At the same time at a level outside our awareness, patterns of association in another part of the brain (the pre-frontal cortex) is automatically and involuntarily responding to the images in the sensory or perceptual part of a brain. A *pairing* occurs as acquired knowledge about images and feelings are matched with patterns of self-in-relationship. Our unique life experiences, and how feelings and sensory representations have been paired previously, condition this matching. Adult attachment styles, as discussed earlier, would be a good example of this.

We know that the pre-frontal area of the Neo-Cortex is our social consciousness. We have various patterns of self-in-relationship in a state of potential recreation located in the frontal lobes and in turn linked to emotional reactivity in the Limbic System. Memories are not literally laid down permanently in the brain. They exist as patterns that can be potentially re-activated.

A good metaphor for this is a flashlight with a light bulb and a battery. A "C" cell has an electrical potential of 1.5 volts. However, just because it has the potential to generate electromotive force does not mean that the light bulb will be illuminated. For that to take place, a switch must close to complete the circuit. Now electrical current will flow and the light will guide our way.

Habitual representations or patterns of activation are the switches that turn *memory potential* into actual images.

Activation patterns in the pre-frontal cortex fire and a *feeling* sense is related of the outcome to the Limbic System. According to Damasio, and almost all of my clients, this is non-conscious, automatic, and involuntary. These brain regions respond by signaling the Autonomic Nervous System and the body. The result is that our "gut" is put in a state that is most closely associated with the situation in which we find ourselves. This explains why wives or husbands become attachment surrogates. It happens non-consciously, automatically, and involuntarily -- outside of our awareness.

This also activates our skeletal muscles resulting in a portrayal of the emotion on our face as well as establishing a complementary body posture. Meanwhile, the Endocrine System releases hormones that change both the state of the body and brain. Damasio sums the process of emotion by saying, "This apparently exhaustive collection of actions is a massive response . . . it is aimed at the whole organism . . ."

By the time the process is complete, we are in a chemically and emotionally induced trance-state, ready to respond at many levels. This is *emotional reactivity*! What happens next? These huge changes in body and brain are now signaled back to the cerebral cortex and certain other parts of the brain. At this point we are finally ready to "feel" a feeling. In other words, our "reaction" comes to our full awareness.

Before we saw the face of our friend, we had a sense of "self." The massive process caused by seeing our friend creates another image of the *self* being impacted by those images. Damasio sees this as a juxtaposition of the two states and labels it "the self perturbed." It is very likely that it creates an interference pattern much like a holographic image from a laser beam.

How we are *feeling* arises out of this image of being impacted or the "self perturbed." Feeling is a result of the brain's evaluation of *self* and perturbation of *self* i.e. the new Body State, rapidly compared to one another. The combination of the two mind-body states generates the feeling sense of emotions.

Two important points need to be made. The first is that the emotional state generated is below our level of consciousness. In other words, we are not aware of our emotional responses. However, feelings require a thinking process, an evaluation by higher order brain functions. Emotional reactivity resides in the automatic area of the brain - the Limbic System. But we make choices with our frontal lobes. The two are linked together. The problem is for most of us that we are used to allowing our frontal lobes to sleep while letting the Limbic System run our lives as if we had no choice.

Research has shown that the adult brain is wired into the limbic System. So we can't get off the hook that easy! It puts the responsibility back on us to *de-chunk* our thinking process in order to understand why we do what we do. Automatic processes prepare us to respond. Whether or not we stay in the trance is up to us. We have a choice whether or not to respond out of this emotionally reactive state. Whether or not we feel bad or good is a choice. The Paradox of Being Human is that we are compelled to give up choosing freely through the false belief that there is only one response available to a given situation. Just because the old road has deep ruts does not mean that we are forced to use that road.

We do have the choice to stay like limbic robots, or to be free and see the range of choices available to us!

The Birth of Parts

The process of feeling an emotion is simply called "emotional reactivity" or "a reaction." Therefore, a "reaction" is a change in our state of consciousness due to evaluations of changes of self-in-relationship. In other words, a reaction is a feeling along with a state of preparedness in response to what we perceive is happening to us. I'm not assuming there is an automatic linkage to behavior, although we can easily understand that reactivity is all about preparing our bodies to respond or behave in a certain way.

Let us assume for a moment that seeing our friend's face generates an all too familiar anger. We respond by making a sarcastic remark. The same processes outlined above allow us to evaluate our behavior. We might say, "I hate it when I get sarcastic like that!" We are noticing our reactivity and condemning our negative attitude. I referred to this in an earlier chapter when I talked about "hating the *part* that hates."

So for each reactive state we generate we create other states of *self* that evaluate the reactivity and form a "goodness" or "badness" value judgment of the reaction. Since our angry *part* is neurologically linked to the *part* making the value judgment, the angry *part* may respond to the *part* that condemns the anger by generating a new response to the reactivity brought up by the self-condemnation. This new reaction may be to justify the anger. The justification may be internally criticized by the other *part* causing another justification. This circular internal reactivity eventually results in polarization between these *parts*. If this continues, overtime each *part* will become more extreme in order to balance the increasingly extreme reaction of the other.

We often hear people saying, "Part of me feels this way, but part of me feels that way." They may shift from anger to sadness to happiness, all in a few sentences. In neurological terms, this is all reactivity, which is the result of a *self* that evaluates self-in-relationship and generates a behavioral response. All of this neurological cacophony is the result of Limbic System conditioning. And although higher-level brain functions are involved all along the way, unfortunately the mammalian brain is leading them.

We do not have to be mentally ill to have *parts* of us respond to other *parts* of us. Remember, each reactive state carries with it a mind body trance-state. Reactivity is generated by topographical representations of images that fire areas of the brains sensory cortices. By the time we are responding to the massive shift that occurs from this process, the original perception may well have been lost in the sudden barrage of brain and body chemicals. Attention may be so focused inward that outward changes make no difference to our internal state.

I am going to label the process of matching perception with internal patterns *scanning,* a term I used previously. Further, I'm going to call the quality of being generated from repetitive self-evaluative mind-body reactions a sub-personality or *part*. A *part* has a complete sense of *self* in the process of evaluating changes in mind-body perturbations along with the associated repertoire of behavioral responses. Another way to think of this, based on our earlier discussion, would be that a pattern of activation of self-in-relationship links the frontal lobes to referred responses that reside in the Limbic System. This pattern of activation fires billions of neurons all over the brain when we experience a synchronicity with internal patterns and changes in our self-state. This synchronicity activates a *part*.

We each have a limited number of preferred ways in which we recreate ourselves in this fashion, i.e. activate *parts*. These *parts* are linked to the full range of emotions and feelings. A pattern of activation, after all, is a habitual inclination. We are in the habit of only having a certain number of self-evaluative strategies embedded in the frontal lobes through the repetition of experience in the Limbic System. However, we can create new ones if need arises, especially for self-preservation.

Therefore, we have a modular brain that processes in parallel, simultaneously. This means that we have many potential *selves* or *parts scanning,* ready to re-activate a full-blown persona as a handy way to deal with the world using emotional reactivity. In addition, *parts* develop relationships with other *parts* by evaluating them and their way of being.

Parts Wrap Up

As we stated earlier, our brain cells and neural nets are interconnected. Neural modularity would be interconnected too. *Parts* or modules would be interconnected; be in relationships with other *parts*. How they are interconnected is the subject of the next chapter. Eventually we shall see how *parts* are created, operate on reality, and interact. The most important *part* or *parts* are those that have been disowned, relegated to the *shadow*. All disowned *parts* have their own way of being in the world. This is the most important concept to understand if you are to change your life.

If we look back at our borderline client in therapy, it is easy to see how sub-personalities, *selves* or *parts* are operating - one desperate to avoid abandonment, the other angry and defending. People with Dissociative Identity Disorder experience different *selves* as multiple personalities without being aware of the underlying neurology that creates it. Each has their own distinct way of being, behavior and motivations, even their own physiology. It's not a huge leap to see that we have *parts*, that self-in-relationship is a matter of *multiplicity*.

Through the clinical example of the Borderline, I have shown how *parts* play a major role in our lives. Brain science points in the same direction, and our awareness of our own internal reality should lend some credence to this. Dramatic shifts in personality are a way of life for humans. If you want to see this in action, watch daytime TV. Talk shows tend to reduce participants to their lowest form of self-differentiation. Clearly, we're seeing *parts* in full-blown reactivity.

This chapter then has laid the groundwork for the next step in understanding the paradox in which we humans find ourselves. My goal in discussing Borderline Personality Disorder was to show how theory translates into clinical reality. However, you can prove it yourself. You do not have to have a personality disorder to notice your shifts from being one *part* or another. Aren't we all fun to be with at times and ugly and moody at other times? Do we catch ourselves taking two different positions in conversation every now and then? Aren't many of us aware of a playful *part* and a serious *part* inside of us at the same time?

Watch your friends and co-workers. Now that you have read this chapter, you'll notice them shift back and forth. As they move from one *part* to the next, you may be able to see them defending themselves one moment and criticizing themselves the next. You may notice their pulse and respiration, the color of their skin, or their affect change with the internal shifts.

We shall see that not all *parts* are created equal. Nor do they care about your primary goals and ambitions or your priorities for life. They have their own agendas, and they are "having their way with you." Moreover, you have been a willing participant without even knowing it.

Chapter Five

The Internal System of *Parts*

My first encounter with the concept of *parts* was through NLP, Neuro-Linguistic Programming. Some of the techniques used in NLP involve working with internal *parts*. Overall, the techniques of NLP are aimed at re-mapping the topology of the brain surrounding certain behavioral responses. NLP is concerned with the structure of thought and behavior. There is an overt attempt to "change your neurology." NLP can produce dramatic changes or just subtle shifts in perception and behavior. It is not "talk therapy" where old pain is re-lived, or emotion is released. The idea is to operate, directly or indirectly, on the interior models we use in order to create more choice in response, thereby obtaining different outcomes. One of the most famous concepts used in NLP is eye movement. For example, it was discovered that people look up when they are remembering a visual image. Or they may look to one side or the other, literally looking at their ears. This means they are having an internal dialogue or remembering words or sounds. When they look down, it is a sign that someone is checking out their feelings. Eye accessing queues are enormously powerful in order to understand the internal process that is taking place that generates certain beliefs or behaviors.

Richard Bandler and John Grinder developed NLP after studying the therapeutic techniques of three giants in the world of therapy, Fritz Perls,

Virginia's Satir, and Milton Erickson. Fritz Perls was the originator and developer of Gestalt Therapy. Gestalt Therapy uses the idea that everything is part of a whole. In other words, what is important in therapy is to notice the client's entire unified experience as an expression of what is happening to them. If someone starts tapping his or her foot, it is significant because it's part of the Gestalt of the client's experience.

Virginia Satir was a famous family therapist. Great efforts have been made to codify and map out her techniques as if one could produce a cookbook that would replicate her success. However, what made Satir so powerful was her ability to work with people and express who she was as a person. Nevertheless, Bandler and Grinder were able to distill from her valuable information about rapport, congruence, and her therapeutic techniques that went into the development NLP.

Milton Erickson was the greatest clinical hypnotist that the world has or will ever see. He had an amazing, some would say miraculous, success rate often with patients no one could help. To this day, much of his work remains an enigma since what he did and how he worked was so subtle. Erickson's case studies are among the most fascinating reading in psychological literature.

Erickson

In *Jay Haley on Milton Erickson,* Haley states, "Implicit in Erickson's way of working with patients is the idea that a psychiatric problem is interpersonal in nature. The ways the patient deals with other people and they with him produces his feelings of distress and restricted ways of behaving."

This sounds a lot like self-in-relationship doesn't it? In fact, I believe hypnosis is the bypassing of the frontal lobes or our social models of the world. Hypnosis operates on awareness and perception (or *scanning*). Hypnosis has been called a narrowing of focus or attention. We will see that each of our internal *parts* has the capability to narrow its own focus to only what it sees is important for its own survival.

Erickson would often use confusion to bypass the model of self-in-relationship. For example, once a man walked up to him during a speaking engagement. Erickson extended his arm as if to shake the other man's hand. As the other man responded, Erickson moved his arm down and pretended to tie a shoelace. This was totally unexpected, and for moment, the man had no internal resource to generate behavior. There was no habitual tenancy, no topographical synchronization to reference the behavior. In that space, Erickson made his first inductive command and the man slipped into a trance. Erickson is famous for using many methods to induce confusion that results in a hypnotic state.

Another case involved a man who was afraid to drive out of town. Erickson told him to drive towards the edge of town and pay attention to how he felt. When he felt distress or anxiety, he was to pull over, get out of the car, and lay down in the ditch next to the road until he felt calm. Then he was to drive further and repeat the behavior.

This treatment was successful, but why? Perhaps it made the man feel foolish about his fear so he gave it up. We do not know what Erickson had in mind. In fact, it may not have been important to him to understand why this would work. One thing is for sure. The way in which the man experienced his problem would never be the same after lying for a few minutes in that ditch.

A woman came to Erickson to lose weight. He told her he would help her, but first she would have to gain 20 pounds. The woman protested, but did as instructed and had no trouble losing the weight she originally wanted to lose after gaining the specific number of pounds. Erickson used trance, confusion, paradox, and even confrontation. Ultimately, Erickson caused the patient to discover something they already knew and this previous knowledge led to the cure.

Erickson worked toward change from the first moment of encounter. He was amazing and his methods are still being studied long after his death. In fact, devotees from the psychological community hold a large annual Milton Erickson conference just to study and discuss his work and methods.

Perls

Perls, like Erickson, was not concerned about awareness of the problem's source. Neither Perls nor Erickson cared about early childhood damage to the psyche or if our wife is a metaphor of our mother. Perls wanted us to take complete responsibility for our problems in the present. Perl's Gestalt Therapy is an existential approach meaning that it looks at what's happening in the here and now. Gestalt Therapy is not overly concerned with the past either, but uses awareness of the present as a light to shine on the cause of problems.

If the clients started tapping his or her foot, Perls would then tell them to do it with awareness. In other words, they were to continue to tap their foot and look inside to see what feelings or thoughts were linked to the tapping. He felt anything that happened, even clearing the throat, was significant. His goal was to turn attention to the problem and bring into awareness anything that might be relevant.

Gestalt Therapy addresses *parts* in a couple of ways. First, it defines the problem of internal splitting. This split is the result of what in one's self has been accepted and what has been disowned. Second, what Gestalt Therapy looks for is the "top dog" and the "underdog." The top dog is the internal critical parent. Literally, this internal voice sounds like mom or dad. The underdog plays the role of the defiant, disobedient child.

Often an empty chair will be used to assume these roles. By sitting in one chair and then another, the client talks to and with the *parts* they are playing. It is a way of externalizing the internal role. Chair work is powerful for increasing awareness. Whenever I have done chair work, I have gained new perspectives and insights. When I assume the empty chair in a role-play as one of my parents or as a *part* of me that is disowned I see things I have never seen before. For me, chair work has often been an "ah ha" experience.

Satir and Others

Satir was even more explicit in her use of *parts*. She worked from the position that families teach children to show only some *parts* of themselves while the rest lay below the surface. According to her teachings, parents and society teach us to be placating and call it "being nice." She states that we are taught to blame others and call it "assertiveness." We substitute super-reasonableness for objectivity and irrelevance for spontaneity. All of this creates incongruity in our communication and consequently in our relationships.

Satir used a specific technique called a "parts party" to assist in the process of integration of "good" and "bad" *parts*. Her techniques acknowledged that *parts* are in conflict with one another and that ignoring, denying or distorting *parts* only reduces possibilities for growth.

Other therapies use the idea of *parts* or roles. Transactional Analysis is an example. Eric Berne's T A is based on the idea that at any given moment in time, we are operating from either an adult, a child, or a parental ego state, and transactions between people are interactions of these shifting states.

Using the concept of *parts*, Connie Ray, and Tamara Andreas have done groundbreaking work, which has culminated in a technique called "Core Transformation." This involves direct work with *parts* and has its roots in NLP.

Core Transformation is one of the most dramatic approaches to *parts* work yet. However, there is another school of *parts* work that is more comprehensive, more theoretically complete, and involves the whole person in a systematic way. It is called *Internal Family Systems Therapy*, and was developed by the pioneering family therapist, Dr. Richard Schwartz. His theoretical ideas encompass the entire system of internal *parts*, and include a map for empowerment and self-leadership.

He calls it an internal family system because it is organized very much like our own families. There is no "mommy" *part* or "daddy" *part*, although often *parts* will resemble them or speak with their voices. Because we all grow up in a family system, it makes sense that our early family experiences would serve as the template for our internal system.

It is folly to believe that small children do not develop an intuitive understanding of their family system. They watch what happens, how members interact. They see the family rituals; they hear the family myths. They understand the unspoken roles, they hear the direct and indirect injunctions, and they know about the family secrets.

Children start life by splitting off those *parts* that their parents find unacceptable and they shove those *parts* into the Bag or the Shadow. They go through life dealing with those disowned *parts* by way of parental example. Their heads become full of value judgments about their *parts*. They punish themselves, they act out, and they learn to deny, pretend and lie about themselves. Life's internal struggle begins.

Schwartz's "Internal Family Systems Therapy" holds a comprehensive key to understanding the organization of these *parts*, and how to deal directly with the system of *parts* to bring about balance, harmony, and self-leadership. We will look into this in detail in chapter 7.

Why a System?

Object Relations and Psychodynamic Theories talk about self-objects, introjects, good objects, and bad objects. To introject or to create an introject is to unconsciously incorporate the characteristics of another person or an object into one's own psyche. We have put forth the notion that a *part* is a potential topographical response of the brain to a synchronization of habitual tendencies with inputs from the sensory processors of the brain, which fire patterns of that topology. The resulting recall pattern may or may not correctly match all or even a section of the previously mapped experience. This could result in mistakes or distortions of our perception. It is embarrassing to snap at someone who you feel insulted you only to discover they were not even talking about you!

Objects or introjects sound like they are concrete, discrete brain structures that exist in isolation from other objects or introjects. A self-object, for instance, sounds like a specific neurological knot somewhere that is triggered by some input or memory. However, the concept of *parts* is much more elastic and systemic. We have systems of interacting, interrelated, and interdependent *parts* forming a complex whole. A *part* can cause a body wide response to disturbances in the self-state brought on by both outside and internal neurological activity. The response and associated behavior of one *part* causes a corresponding disturbance in the self-state that is evaluated by other internal *parts*. In simple terms, *parts* are aware of one another. Except under extreme circumstances that are created from life threatening events, *parts* form "relationships" with other *parts*. If life events are too frightening or threatening, the parts that "hold" that experience may be totally split off and we may experience amnesia for the simple purpose of self-protection.

It is widely held that our biological world is a world of systems. Remember the body? We have a respiratory system, a circulatory system, and many different systems that are all interrelated in one large system. We have shown how the neurological structure of the brain is made up of systems of responses, association, and evaluation. At the lowest level of brain processing, our five senses and our internally generated images and feelings trigger internal habitual tendencies that represent images in a certain pattern. If we move to the highest level of brain functioning, these dispositional representations involved an entire set of emotional reactivity, images, feelings, behaviors, and self-evaluations, which present a map of *self-in-relationship.*

Systems theory tells us that systems are hierarchical. In other words, living systems form hierarchies of levels. If we think back to the process of attachment, we can see how this would develop. At the lowest level of brain process, attachment is represented by certain behavioral strategies that create proximity to the caregiver. As the brain grows and expands this basic learning, it becomes recursively related to more complex interaction with caregivers. At first, this is merely sensorimotor in nature. Then proximity is generalized into affection. The process is recursive since as we experience affection it becomes interrelated at the neural network level with our patterns of attachment. If affection is not available, proximity may be generalized into approval, recognition, or some other conditional or value oriented response. Now the first system is linked to the second level, forming a new system with subsystems.

Next, the family system is integrated into this young mind. This level is recursively integrated into the previous system and all other systems that are linked to it. Then we go to school; then we're impacted by cultural messages; then we learn to be a part of society. Layer upon layer of complexity is recursively and reflexively added to the neurological interrelationship. Now the primitive sensorimotor learning is linked to more complex learning that involves language, complete thoughts, and beliefs.

In computer programming, the recursive program is one that calls itself. When we experience an intimate relationship we recursively experience our first intimate relationship, and we express the same attachments style we learned back then.

In systems theory, the term "reflexivity" refers to a brain or an emotional system's ability to activate itself, to evaluate its own results, and literally to look back on itself. We humans are constantly evaluating ourselves. If we weren't, we would never be able to self-criticize.

Along with these ideas is the concept of "circular or causality." This means that systems are not cause and effect or linear, but continuums that lead back on themselves and reinforce homeostasis. Homeostasis is the tendency of a system to stay in equilibrium. Homeostasis is what maintains our system of believing we're still fat even though we may have lost a lot of weight. Equilibrium means that our beliefs, our attitudes, and our way of being in the world are hard to change. No matter what happens our neurological and therefore psychological systems want to stay, or tend to want to stay just the way they are. The net effect is that systems can be hard to change.

If a mother had postpartum depression, the attachment process may have been seriously disrupted and the child may have developed insecure attachment. Let us assume that later the mother recovers and is able to assume the appropriate emotional role of caregiver. The early system of insecure attachment behaviors will be constantly challenged by new positive feedback from the mother. Positive feedback is system lingo meaning feedback that moves the system away from homeostasis toward change. Negative feedback reinforces homeostasis. The ongoing depression would have served as negative feedback reinforcing the system of insecure attachment. However, this new positive feedback will challenge the insecure attachment, changing the pattern of *self-in-relationship* toward a more secure way of relating.

The child will not immediately respond to the change in behavior from the mother since the systems that hold the habitual tendencies in the brain want to stay in homeostasis. It will take some time and many new experiences for more positive interactions with the mother to have an impact on those systems. At the end of early development, both insecure attachment experiences and more nurturing experiences will be recursively and reflexively related to one another. This means that later experience does not wipe out or block out what came before, but is integrated into it.

What has happened is the entire system of self-in-relationship to the caregiver and therefore all relationships with other people will have moved to a level of more complexity. By the time the child is an adult, the system of attachment will be generalized and highly complex.

Let us look back on the mother with postpartum depression. Let's assume that she does not get better, but reinforces the attachment anxieties, i.e., negative feedback. Now the insecurity will be reinforced through negative feedback, calcified, if you will, and the insecurity will be generalized into many other situations as life goes on. Adult attachment situations will lead directly to the expression of innate proximity seeking through primitive behaviors. An infant knows how to rage but is too underdeveloped to express jealousy. An adult will be able to express more complex feelings like jealousy, complete with all of the stories, assumptions, and speculations, but will have restricted behavioral choices.

We stated that systems are complex. Systems tend to evolve and grow, but as they do, they become historically bound to previous states while simultaneously developing new traits as we have attempted to show by example. Systems may even have many separate and different habitual tendencies. These dispositions act in parallel creating multiple interactions (among subsystems of neuron patterns.) There are many simultaneous modes of interaction involving multiple processes and structures. Any single dimension of description is incomplete and would require multiple complementary and irreducible levels of analysis. No wonder we are often left confused and frustrated in our attempt to explain our feelings and behavior. In other words, systems are complicated and do not lend themselves to easy descriptions.

Remember our couple sitting in the restaurant in the earlier chapter? He is accusing her of having sexual thoughts about other men. When confronted with the truth that she is not having those thoughts, he would go into a state of momentary confusion and then go right back in through process of denial then back to the jealousy and acting out anger. In other words, since he has no other way of understanding relationships, a *part* of him that is linked to his early attachment experiences will, once again, become activated. That part will cycle right back through all the same feelings, rationalizations, and justifications much to the complete amazement and frustration of his partner.

That is why *"parts"* is such an easy concept. Although *parts* represent the systems we have described, they also become a metaphor for those processes. As we shall see, the brain has an amazing ability to fill in the story with rich details. When a person describes the *part* of them that generates a certain behavior like jealousy, we can count on the full representation of that personality. We do not have to know the system. The system will be fully represented in the form of images we can see and understand.

As a therapist watching this interaction, I don't have to understand the entire system. I don't have to see its rich complexity. I don't have to know the attachment experiences this person had. I don't have to have a detailed personal history of him or her. I can tell by his reactive behavior that a sub-personality located in his Limbic System is defending an enormous feeling of fear or shame. I know what's happening inside his head merely by watching the interaction of his internal systems or sub-personalities.

In many therapies, the goal would be for him or her to relive early experiences to "work through" the pain. The danger would be actually to reinforce the problem systems. My goal, on the other hand, is for him or her to be able to self-observe internal systems of re-activity- sub-personalities as they interact with one another. Now, he or she becomes the therapist. My goal is that you will be able to do this too.

Chapter Six

Metaphorms, Holograms, Scanning, and Projection

Many therapists use the idea of *parts* in their work with clients. However, most use *parts* as a metaphor for an aspect of a monolithic personality assuming, therefore, that the person has only one large personality. In this book, it is our theory that there is a neurological basis for *parts* and that the idea of only one personality for each person is not supported by brain research. The Paradox of Being Human is an outgrowth of *parts*, and *parts* are an outgrowth of splitting due to value judgments during early development. *Parts* are neurological patterns of personality. However, the way a *part* is expressed is in the form of a metaphor.

The description of *part* becomes a metaphor for the internal process. This is the result of the way we construct autobiographical memory. We literally fill in the blanks when we tell a story about ourselves, and the story we tell of a *part* is a metaphor for the internal process of that subpersonality.

The brain is a "meaning making" machine. We constantly scan for a match between internal meaning and external representations of that meaning. A metaphor is a combination of logical thinking and images. In other words, it is a picture of a deduction about meaning. When we use a metaphor such as, "the boy stood still as a stone," it is nearly impossible for the listener or reader not to generate a vivid internal representation of what the speaker is describing.

If I say, "Work is a meat grinder." I am making an externalization of self-in-relationship to work. "She's an angel," metaphorically describes the quality of self-in-relationship to her. "I feel like a failure," is an implicit comparison. "Life is hard," may not seem expressly metaphoric, but it is expressing an internal feeling in external language. It is comparing a quality of external experience with the change in the state of self through living.

If someone said, "life is difficult;" we would see that "difficult" is an abstraction of real internal experience. If we probed deeper, the answers to explain "difficult" would come in the form of metaphors unless we got more abstractions. "I feel like I've been run over by a truck," for example.

Richard Kopp, Ph.D. in his book, *Metaphor Therapy*, states that metaphors of self and others ". . . structure our personal beliefs, thoughts, feelings, behavior, and relationships in the life situation they represent." He defines three relational metaphors: self-in-relation-to-self, self-in-relation-to-others, and self-in-relation-to-life. He calls the metaphoric structure of personal reality a *metaphorm*. By implication, *metaphorms* actively operate on reality through *scanning* and *projecting*. Kopp also comes close to defining the concept of *parts* as models of self-in-relationship.

The Holographic Part

It is possible to understand parts through the example of laser light. A laser produces a beam of coherent light. If we take a beam splitter and split the laser light into two different beans, we can produce a hologram on a special type of film. One beam is shined on the object to be recorded or photographed and the other is pointed so that it interferes with the laser light bouncing off the object. The film records the interference pattern between the two beams as a hologram. What is important to know about the holographic plate is that there is no picture of an object on the film. There is only an interference pattern.

If we shine a laser through the plate, a holographic image appears. It is a three-dimensional picture of the object originally illuminated and recorded as an interference pattern. They put a hologram on my California driver's license to prevent fraudulent duplication. What is fascinating about the hologram is that if we break the plate into any number of pieces, the image of the object would still appear should a laser be shined through any of the pieces. The whole is contained in the *parts*.

Karl Pribram was studying at Yale as a neurosurgical resident when the hologram was first publicized. He had been working with Wilder Penfield trying to figure out how the brain stores memories. Penfield had done experiments using electrodes touching the brain, which seem to indicate that humans had perfect recall of everything they had ever seen, heard, or experienced in their lives. However, science has shown that memory does not work that way. We re-author memory. It is neither all-inclusive nor "perfect."

Holograms were a blaze of inspiration for Pribram. He saw that the idea of an interference pattern would explain how all of those "perfect" and "complete" memories are distributed all over the brain instead of in little compartments or *engrams* as Penfield had theorized. What followed were Pribram's holographic brain model and ultimately a holographic theory of reality. Pribram postulated that internal as well as external reality was the result of the interplay of holographically coded information. In fact, if he is correct, true reality is unknowable. It is only necessary for the brain to interpret a stream of sensory frequencies and display them holographically for us to "experience" reality. This does not mean that there has to be an objective reality out there somewhere. Nor does it preclude the existence of a "spiritual" side of reality. Pribram concluded that it was possible that our experience of living was similar to a hologram being interpreted by another hologram. What really exists is a fuzzy interference pattern and the laser light of consciousness that creates the image of the world in our head.

Science has now shown that Pribram's ideas may be correct. The process of hearing three-dimensional sound that most of us experience is the result of a reference frequency that exists inside the brain that interacts with the pattern of incoming vibrations. The combination of the two produces our experience of sound. Similar findings have begun to emerge about vision.

In Michael Talbot's book, *The Holographic Universe*, he says, "if the picture of reality in our brains is not a picture at all but a hologram, what is it a holograms of? The dilemma posed by this question is analogous to taking a Polaroid picture of a group of people sitting around a table and, after the picture develops, finding that, instead of people, there are only blurry clouds of interference patterns positioned around the table."

To Kopp, a metaphorm, or metaphor of self and others, is the hologram of consciousness. To Antonio Damasio, consciousness is the attention to an awareness of perceived impacts on self-in-relationship or perturbations of self. Perturbations of self are clearly interference patterns on the neural level. Metaphors, holograms, and perturbations, in essence, described the same process. Certainly, the idea of an interference pattern is consistent with the concept of topographical synchronicity in the brain. The habitual tendencies or *parts* become the laser beams of the topology of the brain.

With this in mind, our experience of reality can be described as *scanning* and *projecting* with the laser beams of consciousness. Each *part* has its own ways of being. Change is the interference pattern that is "observed" by the laser sharp *scanning* of the individual *parts* metaphor of self-in-relationship. For example, the *part* that some would describe as the "inner child" looks at an event from the perspective of how does this impact me and what I believe I want or need.

Imagine the human as a set of neurological laser beams shining through the interference patterns of brain topology. What are produced are internalized representations - pictures, memories, or beliefs, and external *projections*. What we experience is a myriad of holographic images that are patterns of relatedness. Reality becomes a synergy of *parts*, or self-in-relationship patterns, *scanning* for relatedness or synchronicity and projecting patterns looking for a "match." This is how a brain makes meaning and prepares us to respond to our environment. Another word for this process is "perception." Each *part*, however, has its own perception.

Phylogenetic Homology -- The Pattern That Connects

Phylogenetic Homology sounds more like a tongue twister than a helpful concept. Gregory Bateson defined phylogenetic homology as "a formal resemblance between two organisms such that the relations between certain *parts* of A are similar to the relations between corresponding *parts* of B." Bateson was referring to biological *parts*, not psychological *parts*. Imagine a crab and a lobster. Both are radically different crustaceans. Yet, a comparison reveals similarities that could not be found between a dog and tree, for example. We can see claws, eyes that bug out, and other similarities. This is phylogenetic homology.

I believe the same principle applies to our subpersonalities or *parts*. When two people come together in relationship there is an automatic unconscious process of matching *parts*. We call this finding out "what we have uncommon." Can you imagine coming home from a date and saying, "She's awesome. We're so different." No, the first thing we notice is the phylogenetic homology. Since we have different phylogeny, we're not attracted to elephants or orangutans (well, most of us aren't). We are not even attracted to those of the opposite sex that do not have complementary emotional issues. In my experience, introverts are generally attracted to extroverts; fear based people are attracted to shame based people; angry people are attracted to passive people; fearfully attached people are attracted to avoidant people. This is not always the case. However, it happens with predictable regularity.

This explains why people with insecure attachment always seem to find one another and get into stormy relationships. It also explains why, after a divorce, a person may repeat the patterns of the first marriage in the second. The new spouse is psychologically homologus to the first. The word homologus means similar in structure, but different in function. That's why husband or wife number 2 looks and acts different from number 1, and yet turns out to have similar patterns and problems and underlying emotional needs. Sometimes these similarities express themselves in different behaviors, different dynamics, and can be subtle.

But we also know that "opposites attract," or so we're told. I think this is the same process of phylogenetic homology, but it involves our disowned *parts*. Here is where the fun begins in relationships. We will call this process *projection*. However, like introjection, *projection* really is not *projection*. It is a matching of *parts*, of metaphors of self-in-relationship. We think we see inside another person *parts* of ourselves that we have split off, disowned, and banished into the shadow. Since we disowned them in our lives, our *projection* laser beam highlights them in our partners psyche for the same kind of banishment. This means the personal characteristics we fall in love with turn out to be the things we hate in the end. That "free spirit" we married turns out to be the "slob" we hate. How many women have married a man who seemed like the strong, silent hero-type only to discover later that he is boring and emotionally unavailable? Of course, this only happens after the warm glow of infatuation subsides. The judging *part* of us (a *part* that is very much like a parent) that is polarized against the disowned *part* of ourselves will eventually find fault with our partner since we have *parts* with the same qualities (homology).

A good example of this I see all the time with couples in therapy. One partner who is neat and the other is seemingly messy and disorganized. The messy *part* of one drives the neat freak *part* of the other crazy. A mature rational person would see this as a difference in the style and internal organization of each person. However, in the neat freak *part* is trying to banish the partner's messy *part* the same way the neat freak's own messiness was disowned, probably by a critical parent. In other words, the neat freak *part* was created and patterned after a judging parent who also hated messiness.

What is interesting about the neat freak *part* and the messy *part* is that they have deeper symbolic value in each person's life. They may represent constriction and freedom or independence and conformity. In any event, they certainly represent *parts* that are at war inside each person and sometimes at war in relationship with a spouse or roommate or office mate.

This brings up an interesting fact about batterers. Some batterers hurt small animals. Why? Freudian analysis would say through the process of *projection* we see our weak or vulnerable side and defend against it. Phylogenetic homology tells us that small animals are weak and vulnerable just like *parts* of us. They want warmth and nurturing, just as we do.

If every time you wanted nurturing because you were feeling weak and vulnerable your father strapped you into a chair and forced your older brother to beat you, soon you would learn to banish your weak *part*. You would hate that *part*; despise it. You would do anything to stuff it, strangle it, or punish its emergence. After all, keeping your vulnerable *part* in exile would be a condition of staying alive. Those feelings would remind you of how helpless and powerless you were. Any matching of weakness patterns in other creatures would match internal dispositions conditioned to recall the pain of punishment and the fear of death. The *part* that hates your weak and vulnerable *part* and wants to keep you alive steps in and "acts out" a form of the original abuse in a frantic attempt to stamp out the flames of the pain. If you have to kill the little animal to save yourself, you will. This same scenario applies to all of us to an equal or lesser degree. No one needs to be a batterer or worse to attack the *part* they hate in the one they love! We all do this eventually in close relationships.

I have often had people ask me, "How can you work with batterers? Yuk!" They're amazed when I tell them how much I enjoyed being with a group of these men. I get to see all of their subpersonalities. Their behavior cannot be condoned under any circumstances! However, I have the privilege of feeling compassion for them. Compassion for self and others is one of the healing tonics that helps release us from the paradox no matter how egregious our "sins" or mistakes.

Projection, as I'm defining it, is the seeming synchronization between the *parts* of two people. This of course is a trap. I know a man who went through a divorce after a long-term marriage. One of the shocks he underwent was the realization that she was not he. He had so identified with her *parts* that appeared to "match" his *parts* that he had long ago assumed that she was like him. He assumed that she thought as he thought that she had the same values, the same standards, and the same way of looking at the world. What a shock it was for him to realize that she was not an extension of him! She was a different person altogether. Nevertheless, seeing only the matching metaphors blinded him to her uniqueness as a person who was separate from him.

This is called treating a person like an object. Objectification is really the process of assuming, since certain *parts* of others synchronize with our *metaphorms*, they are we. Since they are us, are critical, judging *parts* tear them apart in the same way we tear ourselves apart. A bumper sticker confirmed all of this to me. It said, "Feminism is the radical notion that women are people." Our patriarch society has objectified women for many generations. Now we're busy as a culture objectifying men.

Actually, this applies to all of us. *Projection* keeps us from seeing anyone as unique. It keeps us from seeing the world as anything but a reflection of us. Our natural tendency is for our internal *parts* to project their hologram over everyone to see how we are similar. Awareness or true choice-based living requires the radical notion that even what appears similar is often not similar.

Phylogenetic homology, when applied psychologically, is the metaphor that you must be me so that you can validate me. Moreover, if I have to attack the *part* of you that reminds me of the *part* of me that I have banished or disowned, then I will in order to stay validated.

Scanning and Projection

We have now laid the groundwork for *parts* that *scan* and *project*. They *scan* only to perceive those things that might activate "their version" of reality. They *project* to justify their point of view by seeking others of like mind.

Misery loves company. Alternatively, they *project* so that they might operate on the world to deny the existence of other *parts* whose sense of self they do not want to re-experience.

Another way of looking at this is through the lens of value judgments. Damasio points out that the body is the "theater" of the mind. "By dint of juxtaposition, body images give to other images a quality of goodness or badness, of pleasure or pain." His major idea is that we all have an "as if" mechanism that allows us to simulate emotional body states to get a "gut feeling" as to the "goodness" or "badness" of a perception, thought, or idea. He calls it his "Somatic Marker Hypothesis."

According to Damasio, what starts as an innate process to keep us alive evolves, through the process of experience, into a repertoire of things categorized as "good" or "bad." ". . . the ability to detect good and bad things grows exponentially. The problem becomes one of disposition. If a new concept of the world is *part* of the scene where the previous concept was labeled good or bad, association will label the new component even though there is no innately preset value for that item." In other words, we generalize the ability to make value judgments about everything. If a husband or wife gets inadvertently associated with something else that has been labeled "bad," he or she is also labeled "bad."

Scanning and *projection* are value charged. *Parts* have a value agenda. As long as *parts* are perceiving and acting in their (limbicly) conditioned style, our mind will be filled with the value - the "goodness" or "badness" of everything all the time. Every thing, person, or situation will be immediately labeled "good" or "bad," a "blessing" or "misfortune," a "blessing" or a "calamity," "good" or "evil," "right" or "wrong." What started as survival mechanisms turns into value judgments run amok.

Chapter Seven

Your Internal Family System of Parts

Discovering the paradox is very close. The concept of *parts* was by necessity established first because it is one of the *parts* that we carry inside of us that creates The Paradox of Being Human through the specific way in which it *scans* and *perceives*. However, since a person cannot be free from paradox without adjusting the entire internal system of *parts*, all of them must revealed.

By now, you have had a lot of time to think about your personal history and how it may have affected the automatic processes located in your Limbic System. It was necessary to go through all of that in order to come to these next chapters. As we go through the description of the various *parts* and their functions, try to personalize the information as much as you possibly can. Each person has his or her own special, individualized version of what we're about to discover. The key to freedom and release from the Paradox is in getting to know your internal system of *parts*. It is the goal of this book to put you in charge of them. Just as in theory, the Limbic System has been in charge all along, long before the frontal lobes had anything to say about it, you have not been in charge of your *parts*. The goal is to put you in the lead giving you new perceptions and behavioral choices.

In this chapter, we will describe Richard Schwartz's Internal Family Systems model. Try to keep your *parts* calm as you read the chapters that follow. Let them know it is not my intention that they be killed, put out of business, or disrespected in any way. This is a concern for many clients when they come to therapy. Our *parts* believe they are performing a valuable service for us. Our lives may not work very well because of them, yet they deserve respect, and need to know no one is out to annihilate them. Nor will one *part* be allowed to get the upper hand over another *part*. The ultimate goal is self-leadership, balance, and harmony.

The Myth of the Simpletons

In his book, *The Evolution of Consciousness*, Robert Ornstein refers to our *parts* as simpletons. "The mind is a squadron of simpletons. It is not unified, it is not rational, and it is not well-designed - or designed all." He confirms that emotional information is fed through the Limbic System that may not allow conscious control of the emotional re-activity of our *parts* unless we learn to intervene. In fact, many sources now confirm that reactivity travels through much faster neural pathways than does conscious cognition. In other words, it is easier and quicker, milliseconds faster, to be reactive then to make behavioral choices. This ability came in handy when it came to running from a Saber-Tooth Tiger without stopping to think first. Our ancestors needed this gift of functioning to escape danger with their lives. Unfortunately, in humans, it allows us to get angry with our parents before they're finished saying, "Hello." Ornstein says that everything goes through our "world processor." " . . .what comes out are a few features of the world, features that usually kick off our reactions and our percepts." This sounds analogous to what we have called *scanning*. Ornstein confirms this. "The neural underpinnings of the mind evolved in part to select only that which is of use to survival . . . so we have sets of simpletons who select their bit of the world, fight for control, and act in a way that helps us . . . we dream up our conclusions about the world . . . Reaction and judgments originally evolved for emergency work...swap in and out of consciousness, bringing about distortions."

In the chapter called "Getting to Know 'Yous,'" Ornstein sums up the human condition. "There are so many simpletons going about their business that it is no wonder that our mental system evolved to keep us out of touch with them all and to interpret ourselves in a simple way."

According to the Moslem and Sufi tradition, *parts* are called *nafs*. In Robert Bly's book, *The Sibling Society*, he says that *nafs* are greedy, dictatorial, and tyrannical commanding us to do "wrong." The *nafs* fit right into what Bly labels the Feeding, Sexuality, Ferocity System, Bly's term for the Limbic System or mammalian brain. Bly has a low opinion of the *nafs*. He says that they feel that they are God and ". . . express no fear of God." The Apostle Paul confirms this in Romans 8:7 " . . . because the mind set on flesh (carnal mind - Limbic System) is hostile toward God; for it does not subject itself to the Law of God, for it is not even able to do so . . . "

We shall see that all of these ideas are true of *parts*. They can be nasty little simpletons. The problem of personal change and increasing choice is not solved, however, by condemning the *parts* as simpletons or as unwanted, or as disowned. Ornstein and Bly evidently want to bemoan the Limbic System just as Paul did 2,000 years earlier. But we have learned something of ourselves over the millennia. The Limbic System through connections with the Frontal Lobes may be the Feeding, Sexuality, Ferocity System. Nevertheless, *parts* are part of us. And we have already seen the unwelcome results of disowning or exiling *parts*.

This means there is something we can do that will change our relationship to our *parts*, validate our own feelings instead of condemning ourselves for even having feelings. *Parts* are powerful internal resources that have been waiting most of our lives to help us. *Parts* have a positive self-intention. Condemnation, shunning, stuffing, or punishing those strong feelings only makes the chorus yell louder. One sure way to make a child scream is to tell them to be quiet and then hold your hand over their mouth. Acknowledgment and validation will cause dramatic shifts to occur in the internal system of *parts*. Their behavior will suddenly change when they discover you care about them, when you start caring for yourself.

The Human System

A child is a system of *parts* embedded in a larger system; the family of origin. In the early chapters, we saw the splitting that takes place that creates the *parts* and forms the internal system. If the external system in which the child is born is not healthy, the internal *parts* of the child will arrange themselves to "cope" with the pressures of the family system. This means that *parts* will be constrained from performing their preferred roles and that valuable internal resources will be diverted to "cope" with the external pressures based on that family's particular value judgments.

I had a client who had a *part* that was hard and cold, totally devoted to surviving a horribly abusive childhood. Physical and emotional abuse had started by age eighteen months. Consequently, this part was huge and dominated her entire internal system. The problem, she realized, was that all of her motivational power and energy was tied up in this part that was trying to help her survive. Of course, as an adult, the threat had passed. In fact, her abusive parent was dead. Yet, all of her energy was diverted into surviving the abuse that had ceased years ago. It became a vital part of her therapy to move that part of her toward its preferred role in her life so that her passion and personal power could be directed toward her current life goals.

As we have stated, massive brain development proceeds in a child after birth; wiring, pruning, and rewiring neural connections as learning about the outside world continues. This adaptation involves the child's self-concept, self-worth, and how he or she values their sense of uniqueness. Pressures from the family system constrained neural development. *Parts* then develop along the lines of these constraints. *Scanning* (looking for one, narrow, predetermined version of reality) replaces actual perception, reactivity replaces behavioral choice, and frustration and worry replaced freedom and creativity.

Richard Schwartz, who developed Internal Family Systems Therapy, also states that trauma or "burdening," will throw the internal system out of balance before it's fully developed. Trauma forces the internal system to adapt immediately whereas burdening is adaptation due to the constant pressure over time of being embedded in a dysfunctional system. We have already seen some of this in the case of insecure attachment, the borderline personality, and batterers. It is important to see the distinction here. Many therapies would point to early trauma as creating damage or intra-psychic wounds. Schwartz instead would say that pressures to cope distort the system of internal resources. The system of *parts* becomes imbalanced and polarized. The concept of "imbalance" and "polarization" are a radical departure from the concept of" wounds" or "damage."

The result of burdens the system accumulates along the way is that *parts* of the system become frozen or fixated developmentally at the time of the trauma or burdening. Schwartz says, "These frozen members not only are no longer available to help, but their extreme emotions further constrain the system and forced other members into hyperprotective roles. The child, otherwise borne with the resources for balanced and harmonious living, is now developed to cope with perceived external threats and violent internal strife."

Balance, Harmony, and Leadership

Besides development, there are three aspects of human systems that are vital to our understanding of the Paradox. The first has been alluded to already, *balance*. Each part in a balanced system should have equal voice in decision-making. Take the workaholic, for example. Here is a person whose playful *parts* or whose tired *parts* never get a say in decision-making. The *part* that is the workaholic is frantic to stay away from certain feelings of insecurity and "dominates" other *parts* when it is time to decide what to do, work or play.

Another aspect of balance that Schwartz has identified is access to resources. In a family, if the father is the only one who can spend money without being questioned, then others are restricted from that resource. There are internal resources as well. In a balanced internal system, all *parts* have access to resources.

What about responsibility? In a family, everyone must be responsible for their actions and behavior. In the internal family, the same applies. We shall see that there are *parts* that insist on taking responsibility for other parts. This actually constrains both *parts* and leads to imbalance.

The last dimension of balance is the concept of boundaries. Boundaries are what define one system from another, one *part* from another or one person from another. In a family, boundaries distinguish one person from another. Boundaries establish the mother and father as the "executive subsystem" of the family. Often this boundary means there are rules regarding access to their bedroom. An example of a boundary violation is a toilet with no lock on the door. This lack of privacy also implies that certain family members can have their boundaries violated. Incest, for instance, is not only a crime; it is a boundary violation.

Another way to look at a boundary is to define it as the place where "I stop and you begin." Think back to the earlier chapter where we discussed the 35-year-old son who could not leave home because he was being used as emotional support for his mother. This is a boundary violation, a merging, an enmeshment. There is no distinct boundary for emotional intimacy.

Imagine a marriage of two people as being two circles. In a healthy marriage, these two circles are going to merge or overlap slightly. In other words, the boundaries between the two people are somewhat diffuse. In an unhealthy relationship, the circles will overlap to a much larger extent. This means that one person sees the other as nothing more than an extension of him or herself. Of course, there is the other extreme where the circles do not overlap at all. This is an example of the rigid boundaries. Boundaries that are either too rigid or too diffuse are warning signs of a troubled relationship.

When working with *parts*, we see the same sort of boundary issues. The most common way in which this is manifested is with what Schwartz calls "blending" and masquerading. Blending happens when a part of us is activated and takes over the *self*. We would typically see this when someone gets angry and begins to act out the anger. Masquerading happens when a part pretends for long periods that they are the real *self*. The more blending and masquerading that goes on with a person the more unidimensional they appear - flat and predictable. Peoples whose *parts* have some boundaries always appear more interesting and multidimensional. Some people may seem interesting at first only to become boring and irritating because their "act" never changes and wears thin after a while. Boundaries lead to internal harmony.

Harmony is not a hard concept to understand. In the family, harmony exists when each member respects the other. They work cooperatively together and at same time value and support differences. By doing so, each member is able to "fit in" to his or her most valued role in the family system.

The internal system is similar. Harmony exists in the internal system of *parts* when each part understands the other. *Parts* that respect, and I dare say understand, the positive *self*-intentions of each in performing their roles in the system promote an internal atmosphere of peace, harmony, and *self*-acceptance.

It is easy to see a person who has the opposite of harmony at work in their heads. Schwartz calls this "polarization." Polarization is a result of two *parts* that do not approve of one another. They do not like the other's behavior and, therefore, become extreme in their attempt to offset that behavior with extreme behavior of their own. A good example of this happens all the time in therapy. A client will suddenly experience deep emotions and begin to cry. While one part of them is experiencing sadness, another part will speak through the tears of the first saying, "I can't do this! I told myself I wouldn't cry. I hate it when I cry."

One of my early encounters with this was a man who had two "little boy" parts. One was a risk taker who wanted to explore and have fun. The other was insecure and needed to stay close to "mommy." Whenever this man left his apartment, the insecure little boy would give him an intense feeling of anxiety, forcing him to get back to a feeling of comfort by returning home.

Meanwhile, the adventuresome boy became increasingly angry and impulsive. This led to episodes of somewhat erratic behavior. The problem was that the insecure boy seemed to win out most of the time. Not only that, but the "tied to mother's apron strings" behavior had been generalized. In his youth, he had learned to gain mom's approval by staying close and keeping a low profile. Of course, his behavior never got him the responses from his mother that he needed. Later, as an adult, he did the same thing metaphorically. He would keep a low profile and do a good job. He was passed over for promotions, and finally laid off. He was enraged since he had done what he was supposed to do, but no one had noticed.

There is a good chance that his clinging behavior started in the attachment phase of infancy and gradually evolved into a lifestyle with the paradoxical injunction, "be invisible in order to get recognized."

You do not have to be a therapist to see polarization in people. Listen to yourself talk. How often do you hear yourself criticizing what you have just said in the same sentence?

"I'd love to take a vacation right now, but that would really be a stupid thing to do!" "I look good in this dress, but I need to lose a few more pounds." "Roy is a great guy, but he's so quiet it makes me crazy." If you watch your friends and associates carefully, you will the see them shift in affect or the emotional content of what they're saying, when these polarizations are vocalized. You are literally seeing two *parts* that are polarized competing for airtime.

"I really tied one on last night. I know it was a stupid thing to do, but it sure felt good. I'm going to have to learn not to do that." It's as if there is an internal group constantly monitoring the comments of each, making interjections, and responding to one another. You can see ecological changes occur as these different *parts* move into and out of the conversation. One way to monitor this is by watching eye movements.

Probably the biggest contribution made by NLP was the discovery that eye movements map our access to different types of brain images and processes. As mentioned before, when a person looks up they're remembering a visual image. When they look to one side or another, as if they're looking at their ears, they are either having an internal dialog or remembering an auditory experience like listening to their mother's voice. When they look down, they are experiencing a feeling. When a person is looking straight-ahead and de-focusing, they are visually constructing an image "out there" in space.

There is much more to eye movement cues. For example, looking up left or right can have different meanings depending on hand dominance. When it comes to *parts*, polarization and who is speaking, the eye movement cues can tell us about the internal shifts we are observing. For instance, one example contained the phrase "I need to lose a few pounds." If the person's eyes shifted to the left laterally as they said those words, I would speculate that they were accessing a remembered auditory experience in their non-dominant hemisphere. In other words, there's a good chance a portion of what activates this part is the remembered critical voice of a parent.

Polarization is our main source of misery. We can learn to tell who is speaking just by the way they use the words. This will lead us to exercise a new level of awareness and act on our own internal system. Schwartz would call this *self*-leadership. Whenever we differentiate ourselves from our emotions, our true *self* is in the lead. Some psychologists call this "differentiation" of *self*.

Many years ago, as I read *The Origin of Consciousness in the Break-Down of the Bicameral Mind*, by Julian Jaynes, I was struck by the notion that we humans had taken an evolutionary step forward with the development of the Neo-Cortex. Nevertheless, all we have really done with that, other than learn to speak languages and so forth, was to stand back and complain about our Limbic System. "I hate it when I do that!"

It was as if suddenly we had *self*-awareness, but all we could do with it was to complain about our own reactivity and lot in life. Paul talks about this struggle in Romans 7:15 "for that which I'm doing, I do not understand; for I'm not practicing what I would like to do, but I'm doing the very thing I hate." He talks about the Limbic System in verse 23. "But I see a different law in the members of my body, waging war against the law of my mind, making me a prisoner of the law of sin which is in my members. Wretched man that I am! Who will set me free from this body of death? . . . on the one hand I myself with my mind am serving the law of God, but on the other, with my flesh, the law of sin."

This certainly sounds like polarization between *parts*. Fortunately, for us, there is a way out. This is what Schwartz calls "leadership." It is clear reading Paul that he is struggling mightily with those *parts* of him that will not serve his higher purposes. For eons, man had done the only thing about this it appeared he could do. Take those offending *parts* and punish them, stuff them, banish them, and hate them. This is polarization, not leadership. All of those *parts* have a positive *self*-intention. Rather than listened to their message and accepting our various selves, we disown them forcing them to scream louder and "act out" in order to get our attention.

Leadership means activating our true *"self"* and not accepting a masquerading part as a *self*. It means loving those *parts* of us that are weird, and firmly making new decisions while taking care of the needs of our inner ensemble.

Our sense of self-in-relationship is a function of the frontal lobes, and, as we pointed out in an earlier chapter, it is not fully developed until we become teenagers. It's little wonder that the *"self"* takes a back seat to the *parts* that come out with all that re-activity from the Limbic System. No one ever told us that we had a choice. There are no parental or cultural maps that explain that we are not our *parts*. So by the time we achieve self-awareness certain of our *parts* have been running our lives for years. *Parts* have either masqueraded as a *self* and pushed the *self* into the background, or *parts* have blended with the *self*, stealing our ability to lead our own internal system.

Internal Family Systems Therapy has a presumption that the *self* is not damaged, has not disappeared, or is not crushed, fractured, or shattered. The real problem is that in most of us, the *self* has allowed the more intensely emotional *parts* and pretending *parts* to assume leadership. Our true *self* has been co-opted, constrained, and overwhelmed by our emotional reactivity and our attempts to deny those outbursts.

There is a true *self* in there somewhere. It exists in the frontal lobes. If we gradually coax it to the forefront and get the *parts* to cooperate in allowing the true *self* to lead, we will find that the system is naturally motivated toward mental health. *Parts* learn they no longer need to be extreme in order to be heard. Once this happens, it can be like a miracle, behaviors can change dramatically. Even persons with severe symptoms of personality disorders can achieve a permanent shift toward balance, harmony, and leadership.

We will meet this true *self* in a later chapter. I call it the *Meta-Self*. At the core, we all have a place from which we observe, experience, and interact with our *parts*. *Self*-leadership is the road map that turns misery and complaining into action that can address imbalance, polarization, and blending. We can learn to trust ourselves and stop identifying with our *parts*. We will see that *parts* respond quickly to *self*-leadership once the *self* is differentiated from the *parts*.

However, before this can happen we must meet the *parts* "up close and personal." So, let us meet the Managers, Firefighters, and Exiles!

Chapter Eight

Managers, Firefighters, and Exiles

Richard Schwartz's *Internal Family Systems Therapy* recognizes three types of internal *parts*: Managers, Firefighters, and Exiles. That is not to say that we all only have three *parts*. But we only have three "types" of *parts*. Exiles are those *parts* that carry the grief of the system. Remembering an earlier chapter, we talked about two developmental questions. The answer to those developmental questions determined whether each of us is either fear-based or shame-based.

Knowing that our caregivers did not want to see or deal with our fear or shame, we had to "exile" it, banish it, stuff it into the bag, and push it into the shadow. The fear or the shame represents our unmet emotional need for security or feeling okay about ourselves. The Exile is created in the Limbic System. At the same time, the split that forms the Exile also forms the Manager. The Manager's job is to strive to meet the unmet emotional need that created the Exile while not allowing us to feel the fear or the shame of the Exile. In other words, the Managers job is to keep the Exile exiled.

There's a *part* of us that is not too happy about not getting our needs met. In fact, on those rare occasions when the Exile escapes, if only briefly, we need to defend against those strong feelings by acting out somehow, thereby protecting the internal system from being overwhelmed by the fear or the shame. The *part* that does this Schwartz calls the Firefighter. He calls it the Firefighter because its job is to "hose down the strong feelings of the Exile."

Let's see how this works in real-life. In her book, *The Battered Woman*, Lenore Walker introduced the "Cycle Theory of Violence." Walker found domestic violence has three phases. We shall see that these phases match Schwartz's *parts* exactly.

The first phase is the *tension-building phase*. During this stage, there is a gradual buildup of anxiety, minor incidents of abuse, and deterioration in the relationship. The second phase is the *acute battering incident*. It is not hard to understand what happens at the stage. Nevertheless, it is more complex than it might seem on the surface. The final phase has come to be known as the *honeymoon phase*. It is during this phase that the batterer becomes contrite, apologetic, and tries to make amends.

Let's shift gears for a moment before we come back to the Cycle of Violence and look at the role of *parts*. Exiles, as the name implies, are those *parts* that are stuffed in the bag, that are banished, disowned, and living in our shadow. Exiles carry the pain in life. They not only carry the pain of abuse, or unmet early needs, but they can be assigned the pain of other *parts* in the system that do not acknowledge their pain. Exiles are usually represented by young children 4 to 8 years old. They are burdened, frightened, and frozen in time. Their reactivity is infantile (crying, complaining, pleading, and complying) and their view of the world is through the eyes of a child. We will come back to Exiles in more detail later.

Firefighters come into existence in reaction to Exiles. Without Exiles, there would be no *parts* in the form of Firefighters. The Firefighters job is to get away from the pain of the Exile. Schwartz labeled them Firefighters because he perceives their function as dowsing out the flames of the Exile's strong emotions. In my view, Firefighters take two forms. Either they defend against the Exiles' pain or they attempt to avoid feeling the pain. Typical defending behavior is shouting, fighting, and any form of aggressive behavior. Defending-type Firefighters are action oriented.

The other form of Firefighter tries to avoid or numb the pain. These Firefighter behaviors include drugs, alcohol, purging, excessive masturbation, promiscuity, stealing and crimes of various types, and suicide. Firefighters force the person out of control and generally frighten or irritate everyone in their lives.

Finally, there are the Managers. The Manager's role is two pronged. First, they must keep the Exiles exiled and the Firefighters from being activated and getting loose. They do this through a variety of strategies designed to keep feelings away. Keeping busy, overwork, distractions, being intellectual, having all the answers, hyper-vigilance, care taking, and over achieving are a number of those strategies.

The second thing they do is pretend that everything is okay and deny to the outside world the horrible truth of the Firefighter's acting out and the discomfort of the Exiles pain. It is hard to tell which the Managers fear the most, Exiles or Firefighters. It's for certain that they fear and hate Firefighters.

Now let us look again at the cycle of violence. Against the backdrop of the three types of *parts* just discussed, it becomes a simple matter to see what is happening from the batterer's point of view. During the tension-building phase, the Managers try valiantly to keep the Exiles exiled. The tension comes from not just struggles in the man/woman relationship, but also the internal struggle between one *part* of the batterer's psyche stuffing the other while the second tries to escape. Since the Exile's pain in the batterer is a result of insecure attachment, shaming by the father, and an abusive early environment, the Managers are fighting a losing battle against a titanic well of hurt and rage.

When the Exile escapes, pain comes close to overwhelming the system. The Firefighter gets loose and batters, using violence to defend against and act out the overwhelming pain. At this moment, we have a picture of horror as the batterer strikes out against the partner. All of the men I've worked with have stated categorically that at this moment they feel helpless, powerless, and completely out of control. They also say they feel under attack. This is a clear example of how *parts* scan and distort reality. At this moment, the batterer is in the grip of the Firefighter who will do anything to defend against the pain. The attachment surrogate, wife or lover, is the perceived source of pain and so the counter attack begins.

Controlling behavior is the result of feeling out of control. Oddly enough, using physical or emotionally abusive power is a manifestation of feeling powerless. Aggression is an act of helplessness. Once Exiles get loose, the feelings are so powerful that Firefighters conclude they need to be extreme beyond reason to deal with the pain. They really feel that they will die if they don't stop the pain they are trying to avoid. The perceived threat to the self and internal system is that great!

Once the violent incident is over, the Firefighter retreats and the Managers can now assume control again. Horrified by what has happened, they will do anything to keep their partner with them. They apologize, they beg, they promise to change, they buy flowers. A "honeymoon" period really does ensue. Meanwhile, the Managers will steadfastly deny, justify through blaming, and rationalize using distortion the Firefighters behavior. After all, like Exiles, Firefighters are disowned *parts*. The Managers job is to push them back into the shadow and pretend that everything is okay to the outside world.

By the way, there is nearly always another Firefighter at work here, a numbing Firefighter. As stated before, statistics show that eighty percent of all domestic violence involves alcohol abuse. Most of the men I have worked with have been either problem drinkers or drug users.

This may all seem a little extreme for the "normal" reader. Nevertheless, we all, to one extent or another, display these three patterns. We all have a young hurt *part* that comes out, usually when we do not want it to. We all have an angry or rebellious *part* that "acts out" against the pain. This duality explains the love hate relationship so many people have with their parents, especially during the teen years.

In addition, there are the Managers. Managers are those personas that we show to the outside world. They come in many different roles and types. Their main job is to keep everyone from discovering the pain and the embarrassing acting out behavior that defends against the pain. Remember, it is the Manager who cleans up after the batterer during the honeymoon period. It is the Manager that must apologize after getting drunk at the party the night before. It is the Manager that usually, but not always, masquerades as the person's self.

We have said that *parts* are frozen in the past, burdened, and forced into extreme roles because of polarization with other *parts*. Because of this, *parts* are constrained in their behavioral responses to a given situation. Each *part* thinks it can do only one thing. *Parts* think there are no behavioral choices, there is no freedom to think and evaluate differently. There is only reactivity. Each *part* only knows how to respond with one behavior! Through awareness, we can move away from the reactivity of *parts* and experience a myriad of choices in any given situation.

Managers

As we have stated, Managers live in fear of the escape of the Exiles for this means they must deal with Firefighters. In therapy, Managers are the first barriers to getting anywhere with the client, since therapy is designed to get at "feelings." It is necessary for the Managers to trust the therapist before they'll allow entry into the system. Different Managers have different ways to protect the system. However, it is vital for the purposes of change for us to understand that Managers feel they are forced into these roles. They do not enjoy being managerial and would rather be doing something else if they did not think it was so necessary for them to be Managers.

Most people have a Manager that tries constantly to stay in control of situations and relationships. Many times this is done through being highly logical, needing to be the expert, or having all the right answers. This is not fakery. We all know people who are extremely confident, who have a mind that stores vast numbers of factoids, who can solve complex problems. I have labeled this type of Manager the Librarian, the Controller, or the Know-it-all.

This *part* or another similar Managerial *part* may be the Striver or the Achiever. This Manager wants the person to accumulate money, a list of achievements, or a position of power in order to get away from feelings of low self-worth, insignificance, or powerlessness.

In my own life, I discovered a Manager I call the Achiever. My achiever's job was to drive me to so much recognition that I could eventually feel equal to everyone else. In other words, after accumulating a list of accomplishments "as long as my right arm," maybe people would see me as an equal rather than someone unworthy of appreciation. For me, the achiever's task was to create a level playing field so I did not have to feel inferior to everyone else. Seeing this was a tremendous revelation, and it opened the path to an exiled *part* of me that felt like "I wasn't much of a person" and not worthy of love. As long as I kept getting acknowledgment, I never had to feel those feelings. As we shall see, this never really works. The paradox was that my achievements merely reinforced my negative self-concept. By the way, it is not unusual for this type of Manager to be the "critical parent" or as Schwartz states "... a bitingly critical task master, never satisfied with performance or outcome."

Perfectionism is an outward display of another kind of Manager. This *part* believes that if the person is perfect in appearance and behavior, they will be loved and excepted. Schwartz calls this Manager the Evaluator.

Schwartz also identifies a Manager that is apathetic and withdrawn. This Manager he calls the Passive Pessimist that tries to avoid risk and situations that arouse anger, sexuality, or fear. This Manager "erodes the person's self-confidence and sabotages performance, so that he or she will not have the courage to pursue goals. . . "

We are all aware of someone who has a Caretaker or Rescuer Manager at work. This codependent person defines themselves through the needs of others. Sometimes this takes the form of being very quiet and good which appears to be extremely passive behavior. Often times a fear-based person will have a Manager that attempts to control other people's feelings or anger by becoming ever so good in a vain attempt to suppress emotions in the other person. At other times, the care taking is more overt. Care taking is always a bargain, however. There is a motive underneath the care taking. The message is "if I take care of you, you must take care of my unmet emotional need." This hidden agenda, which is really a paradox setup between the care taking Manager and its exiled counterpart, can get very sticky and gooey for the person being taken care of. They may feel manipulated but not know why.

Then there are Worriers and Dependent Managers. Worriers are obsessed with the worst-case scenario and Dependent Managers are obsessed with being victims.

There is another Manager, the Denier. They distort reality to ignore what they do not want to see or hear. I had experience with a denier recently. The denier's wife had been talking with great concern about her stepson, the denier's son by a previous marriage. The wife was very concerned and went on at length, finally asking for my advice. I suggested that they might join a group of other couples with blended families. That way they could interact with other parents with the same concerns and experiences. Throughout this conversation, the denier husband sat silently. When his wife left for a moment, he turned to me and gestured toward the view from the patio where we were seated. "Great view," he observed.

The wife returned and engaged in more animated conversation about her stepson. Finally, the denier turned to her and said, "Let's go home and see that movie."

There are a couple of interesting observations to be made here. Obviously, the denier was going to do anything to avoid the feelings around the situation with his son. Less obvious was the fact that the Denier/Manager in the husband was activating a caretaker *part* in the wife. This is the key to understanding unhealthy relationships. In this case, it serves both people to be activated in this way. The Denier has an agenda that can be served by the wife's Caretaker. The wife has an agenda that is being served by the husband's *part*. She is able to be a caretaker to her stepson so she doesn't have to experience her own feelings that are exiled through care taking, probably feelings of abandonment. Deniers and caretakers are often not the best of parents. The son is the ultimate loser. The Denier will deny the son's reality while the Caretaker care takes to fulfill her own emotional needs, which have nothing to do with her stepson.

The final Manager that Schwartz identifies is the Entitled One. Entitlement is a substitution for empowerment. The Manager who is entitled urges the person to grab what ever they can for themselves without regard of the consequences to self and others. I once had a client who had a Manager who was entitled. Every time the woman got any amount of money, the Entitled One would force her to spend it all on lovely things because she had been deprived all her life and deserved to be surrounded by nice things. Unfortunately, this had a devastating effect on her financial situation and kept her unable to meet her economic needs.

No wonder Managers would rather be doing something else. On the one hand, they take on the responsibility for the safety of the entire system. They must scan the outside world for situations that are perceived threats to activate an Exile. On the other hand, they must keep the lid on the Exiles. It gives us a picture of the traffic cop in the middle of a busy intersection with one hand up holding oncoming traffic from one direction while the other hand is holding off traffic from the other direction. It's a constant job that requires enormous energy and vigilance. It is exhausting. By mid-life, our primary Manager may be so exhausted that the system becomes chaotic. We call this "mid-life crisis."

Firefighters

Firefighters represent the dynamics of the Limbic System. As stated earlier, our emotional reactivity comes from habitual tendencies in the brain. Emotional reactivity is quicker than cognition by milliseconds. Firefighters flood the body with strong chemicals. They put us is a state of readiness. Left unchecked, a Firefighter will activate a pre-disposed response and we "act out." Acting out is the same as defending against feelings, but it suggests an immaturity and a lack of consciousness or awareness. I had a teacher in graduate school who said, "What doesn't get worked out gets acted out." Children, who are often unable to tell us what they're feeling, will display feelings through their actions. Depression, trauma, and anxiety can all be seen in the acting out, or naughtiness of a child.

In adults, Firefighters are impulsive, attacking, angry, and oriented toward motion and action. But, as stated before, this action can also serve to numb, distract, or dissociate. Schwartz also points out they can be self-soothing. Strangely enough, self-mutilation or self-inflicted pain is a form of self-soothing. Pain that one can control often takes on an ecstatic fascination. It is more desirable than pain that feels out of control. Rocking the bed and thumb sucking are forms of self-soothing in children. Children will grow out of this but I wonder what self-soothing "acting out" replaces rocking the bed as a person gets older.

Other self-soothing activities may include compulsive behaviors like excessive hand washing. Compulsion is a defense against shame or anxiety. The belief is the more my Firefighter washes my hands the further away from those bad feelings I get.

I once had a client who would get panic attacks whenever she drove on a Los Angeles freeway. Maybe that's a healthy response. Nevertheless, it became clear during therapy that what triggered her most was when other vehicles, especially large trucks, got too close to her. The *part* of her that gave her panic attacks was attempting to keep her from being emotionally hurt. The freeway was a metaphor for her internal system. Her Firefighter was hosing down the strong feelings of hurt that happened when people got too close.

She had had an extremely abusive home life during childhood and as a result had stopped showing any affection toward her husband. When he filed for divorce and moved out, she was relived since the pain of being close was far greater than the pain of being alone.

There can be great comfort in contemplating suicide. Some Firefighters will go beyond mere suicidal thoughts to the actual life taking itself. The power and danger of Firefighters should never be underestimated. Firefighters will do whatever is necessary to hose down the strong feelings of the Exile.

This also explains indulgence in crime, the exhilaration of breaking the rules, and the protectiveness of rage. The shame or fear of the Exiles can be seen as such a great threat to the system that Firefighters must become ever more daring in their efforts at taking the person away no matter what the cost.

Sometimes it can be difficult to see the difference between a Firefighter and a Manager. One way to see this is to reference when the *part* was activated. Managers function before Exiles escape - keeping the lid on the Exile. Firefighters are always activated after Exiles escape. One of the rules I use with my clients is that they can not just say they are angry. Angry fire fighting is always the result of the escape of an Exile. This means there is always a feeling primary to anger working just below it. In fact, the rule I use is that the anger is only as big as the pain that triggers it.

Therefore, Firefighters always are activated by the Exile's escape. What can make this difficult to stop is how quickly this can happen. The escape of the exiled *parts* happens so quickly that only a small dose of those emotions activates the Firefighter. Nevertheless, the pain is always as big as the anger even if the pain is mostly out of consciousness.

Exiles

It may occur to some to ask how many *parts*; Exiles, Firefighters, or Managers, do we have? It varies according to trauma, our family system's value judgments, and the stress of growing up during critical developmental periods. All people, as we saw in earlier chapters, have exiled *parts*. This makes the function of Managers and Firefighters necessary. Even "normal" people will have a system defined by these three *parts*. A group of three to five *parts* is typical. However, the more dysfunctional the family of origin or the more severe experiences that occur in childhood, the more *parts* are necessary to deal with all that toxicity.

In his book, *The Mosaic Mind*, Schwartz and co-author Regina Goulding deal with the case of a woman who experienced severe sexual abuse as a child. Coping with this kind of burdening created an ensemble of twelve *parts*. One of the *parts* presented as a young child who refused to be identified and was assigned to carry the horrible memories of abuse, the knowledge of which was barred from the rest of the system. It is important to know that this woman had been diagnosed as having a borderline personality disorder instead of multiple personality disorder. She simply did not have the constellation of symptoms associated with in MPD (now known as DID, Dissociative Identity Disorder).

As we have seen earlier, Exiles are formed when, as children, we discover that our pain and terror are not going to be validated or cared for. Our parents react to our pain the same way they react to their own Exiles, that is, by being Managerial instead of human. We Exile our pain and fear and the internal polarization that sets off the paradox in each of us begins.

Exiles feel unloved, unacceptable, shamed, fearful, and guilty. They have needs that are never fulfilled, but they try throughout their lives to break out of their exile to get what they want. Increasingly, since the person refuses to hear their Exiles, Exiles become indirect communicators. They give us nightmares, flash backs, or reveal memories suddenly. They burst forth with huge feelings at times when we are weak or when showing feelings would be inappropriate.

Of course, the more this happens, the more the Firefighters become extreme in their attempt to douse the feelings. The Managers become more determined to stuff Exiles and more critical in their evaluation of both Exiles and Firefighters. Exiles respond by protesting ever so much more strenuously whenever they get an opening. Thus, polarization between *parts* begins and the internal system becomes extreme.

In their state of distress and neediness, Schwartz says that Exiles can even endanger the person. They do not perceive the present circumstance of the person. Their scanning is based on being five years old or whenever they were burdened. Five-year olds are not sophisticated thinkers. They do not understand that flooding the self with overwhelming feelings might put them in great physical jeopardy.

This reminds me of one woman in particular who often times would have a reaction when she was driving a car. The emotions would get so big that she had trouble steering and staying straight in traffic. It is not unusual when expressing strong emotions to throw caution to the wind, "fools rush in where angels fear to tread."

Some Exiles might go further and seek a Redeemer. We have all seen certain people who seemed to gravitate to exactly the wrong kind of person, or who attract only those people who can do the most damage. This is clearly true in the case of some women who are attracted to men who are dangerous and physically violent. This is a result of an Exile inside who is seeking to redress the early-unmet need of love and protection. Unfortunately, this person will carry a resemblance to the early caregiver who was incapable of meeting those needs. Exiles sometimes appear to think that they deserve the abuse and degradation of this type of relationship in order to be redeemed and made whole. Thus, they will put themselves in danger of being used, sexually or physically abused, or beaten. Managers have a good reason to fear the release of Exiles.

I recently saw a man in therapy whose mother was extremely dismissing and unfeeling. He had been in a number of relationships with dismissing women. On investigating his *parts*, we uncovered a compliant *part* that was very much like his father. This *part* would become a "door mat" in order not to release the pain of his Exile. He had another *part* that was angry and critical who berated him and told him he was worthless. This *part* seemed very much like his mother. He described his Exile as being a seven-year old boy who was being pulled violently by both parents. He described this Exile as wearing clothes that were torn and shredded from the tug of war. In each of his failed relationships, he had allowed himself to be used financially and emotionally, as well as physically abused.

Another client had witnessed his mother die of a heart attack. His father took the children away immediately and the death of his mother was never discussed. Talk about a burden! Every time his exiled boy came out, he would start to cry. When he talked to that *part*, he discovered the boy just wanted to be held. The burden was the unexpressed grief over his mother's death, not to mention the guilt he felt for watching her die while feeling helpless. A father who appeared cold and threatening had exiled the grief.

The Irony of Parts

There are two extremely important points to be made in concluding this chapter. All of those who have worked with *parts* and the *parts* concept have discovered that *parts* have a positive self-intention. This can be extremely confusing to clients coming in to therapy. They want to be fixed. They want the behavior to change. They want the self-defeating or destructive thoughts to go way. The fact that their sadness or their anger or their caretaking may have a positive self-intention has never occurred them. They just want it to go way. Of course, while all this is happening, *parts* are working in the background saying, "I'm not going anywhere." In other words, although the behavior of a *part* can be maddening and embarrassing, it is trying to accomplish something positive in the life of the person.

The other idea that is intertwined with this is that *parts* are not in their preferred roles. What this means is that Managers do not want to exile Exiles or hold back Firefighters. Firefighters don't like excessive drinking, dissociative behavior, or rage. Exiles don't like carrying huge burdens of pain. All of the *parts* of the system get forced into polarized, burdened, and frozen positions with respect to one another by virtue of what they feel is necessary for the survival of the system. In their view, they are doing what they can for the benefit of the person even though it may seem counter intuitive and counterproductive.

One of the things I have consistently discovered is that angry Firefighters would rather not be angry. Usually they represent the *passion* in the system. Imagine the vitality and passion that would be released in a person's life if their Firefighter *part* no longer had to defend against shame or fear with massive amounts of anger. So if you flip the coin on one side you see anger; on the other side you see passion.

The same is true for Exiles. If you flip over the Exile, you'll often find a *part* that would rather be playful. The same goes for Managers. Often times the flip side of a Manager is a *part* that wants to explore, that wants to be involved. *Parts* are trying to survive. They represent valuable system resources that are constrained from their preferred roles in our lives.

What this means is that hating our *parts* is not the way out of this dilemma. I remember vividly how I came to this conclusion in my own life. I was angry. My anger was out of control. I knew it, my family knew it, and everyone else knew it. When I lost my temper, I (my Manager) would beat myself up for days. I was embarrassed and humiliated by it. In a mild way, I had the cycle of a batterer. The tension would build and I would explode. Usually it took the form of railing against other motorists or engaging in an argument with a customer service operator. Anyone was fair game for my hostility.

I had to learn to love the angry *part* of me. That's right. You see the angry *part* of me was still part of me. It was hard, but I forced myself to make a conscious effort to acknowledge my anger whenever it came up. "Ah, there you are again. Thank you for trying so hard for me. What is it you want to tell me now? What learning is available from my anger? Soon I began to be amused by it rather than embarrassed or sickened. I remember every time I would get angry I would pray to be shown what I was to learn from it. Eventually I had the breakthrough I described at the end of the book.

What I learned was that self-recrimination was not the answer. The way out was self-compassion and self-love. This is a hard concept when you are behaving in an obnoxious manner, and you and everyone can see it. However, re-enacting the abuse that created the original anger only reinforces the pattern of acting out. Our salvation is that *parts* do have a positive self-intention, and through self-leadership, we can get out of the polarization and the reactivity.

Memory

When I was a boy, there was a strong earthquake at about 1 AM, centered somewhere in Montana near Yellowstone Park. We lived in Spokane, Washington, hundreds of miles away from the epicenter. I slept through the earthquake, but my parents did not. They told me that the earthquake had startled them. In those days, we had a drop-leaf dining room table made out of maple. I remember my folks telling me how the swaying from the earthquake had made the table leaves swing back and forth with a banging noise.

I also remembered that my father was going to have hemorrhoid surgery the next day, and per doctor's orders, my mother was giving him a late night enema in preparation for the surgery when the quake it. A few days later, humorous cards began to arrive at the house from friends who had known about surgery. What I remember most vividly was the image of my father lying helpless on the bed as everything in house started to move back and forth. It was a funny image.

The problem with this story is it is evidently not true. Yes, my parents confirmed that there was a quake and there was surgery. They do not remember the dropped leaf table banging away. The odd thing is that in their minds the two incidents are not related. The two events evidently happened on different days at different times. Somehow, I must have linked the earthquake story to the surgery story and rolled them both together.

Even though I like my version of the story better, this does point out how memory can become distorted. The birth of *parts* can be based on this same type of distorted memory.

In his book, *White Gloves*, John Kotre recounts the Watergate hearings. One of the first and certainly most dramatic testimonies came from John Dean who had been White House counsel. He claimed to have had an "excellent memory." His recounting of events in the White House was so detailed that reporters named him the "human tape recorder." As fate would have it, there were real tapes being made of many of those conversations, much to President Nixon's chagrin. Suddenly an opportunity presented itself to find out just how accurate John Dean's memory was. Transcripts of the tapes were compared with transcripts from the hearing. What was discovered was "rampant reconstruction." In fact, Dean's memory as to facts like who sat where in the room and who said what were not even close. In addition, he had made himself more of a central character that he really was. Although wild with distortion, Dean's memory about the big picture of what was happening was accurate. The details were nothing but a guess.

Parts and Memory

Anytime autobiographical memory has been tested. It has come up short. Even memories that are vivid, detailed and repeated with great emotion are not necessarily accurate.

I had a client that represented his Exile as being a boy about seven. He was standing outside of his boyhood home listening to his parents argue inside. He was hitting a large tree in the front yard with his fist in frustration. What I was aware of as I listened was that there may or may not have been a tree in the front yard of his boyhood home. He may never have actually had the experience of hitting his fists on the tree. Also, he may have never actually heard his parents argue from exactly that vantage point.

This memory is a metaphor for the *part* of him that carries the pain. In other words, the *part* is real and so is the description of the *part*, but only so far as it is a symbol of the inner process

There are two points of view about *parts* work. One is that the *part* is really a persona, a subpersonality with its own discrete, autonomous map of self-in-relationship. The other point of view is that the *part* is a metaphor for an aspect of the monolithic personality of the person.

My conclusion about this is that the *part* is, as Schwartz defines it, "a persistent sense of its own singularity or selfhood, autonomous and discrete from other parts within the same person."

In a real way then, a *part* is like a separate person. In therapy, I might treat them like separate people. But the story of a *part* or its autobiographical memory is a metaphor. Because of this, it is vital not to be caught in the content of the story, but to stay in the process of the operation of the *part*. In other words, healing comes from re-establishing balance, harmony, and leadership in the system - not in the accuracy of the details of the pain, anger, and reactions.

We do not know what each person's process will be. For one, the Exiles may have to tell their story of abuse and neglect. For another, it may never be necessary to replay the bad old days repeatedly until the emotions have been "fully discharged" as is done in so many traditional therapies. The *parts* know how to release their burdens and come into the present. We just need to provide the leadership for the system to get unstuck. Yes, it takes coaxing, trust, and patience, but there is no preset formula for each person.

Chapter Nine

The Paradox Revealed

Next to Freud and Jung, Alfred Adler was an enormous contributor to the development of the psychodynamic approach to understanding humans.

However, unlike Freud, Adler viewed humans as being motivated by social urges rather than biological drives. Adler felt that behavior is purposeful and goal directed. Interestingly enough, he felt that consciousness, not the unconscious, was the center of the personality. Adler thought that choice and responsibility, finding meaning in life and striving for success or perfection were the keys to life.

The first six years of life were critical in Adler's view. He believed that at around the age of six a *life goal* is formed. A life goal, according to Adler, is what humans do to overcome feelings of inferiority. This is similar to what a Manager does to try to get away from the strong feelings of the Exile.

Adler was the forerunner of more subjective approaches to psychology and emphasized internal influences on behavior such as values, beliefs, goals, interest, and the individual's perception of reality. His approach to helping people was holistic, goal-oriented, and humanistic.

Adler worked with an individual's "subjective" reality. He felt that what was important was not an objective reality, but how clients react to their perception of reality. In addition, he believed that humans become a unified personality through their life goal. This parallels the idea of Managers masquerading as the *Self*. Adler focused on social interactions rather than on internal psychodynamics.

He coined a term he called "lifestyle," which refers to the individual's basic orientation toward life, in other words a Manager. The lifestyle was the sum of the person's personality and themes of existence. The lifestyle of an individual helped explain how all of the behavioral pieces of a person fit together. He believed that everything a person does is influenced by their lifestyle, which is formed during the first six years of life. He felt that **it is not one's childhood experiences that are crucial, but one's present interpretation of those events.**

The most significant and unique concept that Adler proposed he called "social interest." This is an individual's awareness of being part of their family, community, and society in general. Adler felt that the more a person finds their place in the larger society the less of those old feelings of inferiority they would experience. He felt that one's happiness and success rested on feelings of connectedness.

In an earlier chapter, I referred to the thematic nature of our *parts*. I have talked about how the brain generalizes and tries to make meaning. In addition, in a previous chapter *parts* were viewed from the standpoint of emotional reactivity, of having *parts* activated.

Adler gives the key to bridging two concepts, *parts* acting out and having their reactions in the moment and the long-term thematic strategies of *parts*. On the one hand, he says that each one has feelings of inferiority. This sounds very much like a shame-based Exile, which I imagine Adler had. On the other hand, each person strives to overcome those feelings just like a Manager. This sets up, in Adlerian terms, a life goal that becomes thematic or generalized into a lifestyle. In addition, Adler talks in terms of social interest. This is close to the concept of self-in-relationship.

It seems that Adler, like so many, has been fooled into believing that all the strivings of humankind are highly desirable. But striving to overcome "feelings of inferiority" will never achieve that goal. This flies in the face of Adler's thesis that humans become a unified personality by virtue of their life goal. In fact, it is that very striving to meet this life goal causes this "unified" persona to melt down about age 40.

What Adler had actually observed was The Paradox of Being Human. The Exile carries all of what Adler would call "feelings of inferiority." The Manager tries to overcome those feelings. Many examples of this can be seen in real life that demonstrate that this strategy does not work. Presidents, actors, athletes - people from all walks of life that seem to have accomplished great deeds have not overcome their basic fears or shame despite their massive efforts.

The Shadow in Mid-life

Connie Zweig and Jeremiah Abrams edited the book, *Meeting the Shadow*. In the prologue, Ms. Zweig says something with which I strongly identified.

"At midlife I met my devils. Much of what I had counted as blessing became curse. The wide road narrowed; the light grew dark. And in the darkness, the saint in me, so well nurtured and well coifed, met the sinner. . . . I had believed, with a kind of spiritual hubris, that a deep and committed inner life would protect me from human suffering, that I could somehow deflate the power of the shadow with my metaphysical practices and beliefs. I had assumed, in effect, that it was managed, as I managed my moods or my diet, with the discipline of self-control . . . At forty I descended into depression . . . At other times an unknown rage would storm out of me, leaving me feeling depleted and ashamed . . ."

I cannot imagine a better description of the entry into mid-life. Her words are powerful and descriptive, but more importantly, revealing. At mid-life the Managers falter; they stumble. When they do, the Exiles and Firefighters have free rein in a person's life. She even uses the word "manage."

At mid-life the game is up, the Managers are exhausted. People look around themselves and see that life is not working. It is as if they have tilled the ground expecting a bountiful harvest after twenty years of hard work. They finally rest from their toil to take stock and see the ground is as barren as it ever was. Life run by Managers is a barren life.

Some people will go through this crisis unchanged. Others will demand more from life and will reclaim those lost *parts* of themselves from the shadows. They will quell their horror and revulsion of what lurks inside and turn to face it. When they do that, an amazing thing happens. Those *parts* that have been screaming and squirming for years suddenly calm down. Once parts feel heard, they change the way they represent themselves in a person's life..

The payoff for reclamation is wholeness, integration, and health. Honoring the *parts* that live in the shadow allows one to accept their contradictions and to live fully. By now it should be obvious that the human shadow consists of the hidden "Exiles" and "Firefighters." People are willing, however, to let the world see their "Managers" because Exiles and Firefighters just don't make them look good.

Managers can be seen anywhere in all occupations. Many Managers "appear" on TV. Those TV anchors, politicians, and officials sometimes come across like cardboard cutouts of real people. They take themselves so seriously. Maybe it was his innate reaction to the unidimensional phoniness of Managers that prompted the singer Sting to write, "...they all look like game show hosts to me." Managers try very hard to impress, but they fail.

Every time there is a controversy about some issue, the Managers lineup to protect the status quo. Every new discovery or idea threatens the Managers of the establishment with the release of their Exiles. Then all the Managers deny and minimize new ideas, discoveries, and theories. Managers love killing creativity. Someone operating as his or her true self would be open, curious, and inquisitive. Managers want to dig in their heels and refuse to budge. If they considered that they were wrong, their Exiles might be stirred up. This indicates that the "bubba psyche" and the corporate workalcholic psyche are not as far removed as would appear on the surface. They're both up to the same thing. They don't want their Exiles activated.

Businesses are run the same way. People dress up nicely and read the appropriate magazines and newspapers. They parade into the boardroom with pomp and circumstance. All of the Managers are managerial. Then someone lets out an Exile that starts whining and complaining. Next, two people who activate polarized parts in one another start attacking and counter attacking. Finally, the person in charge will, after considering all the facts, allow one of his or her firefighters to be activated by everyone else's anxiety and go into a full reaction. He or she may rant and rave, attack, or become sullen and hateful. Before long, a decision is made that is not rational, makes no business sense, and will be resented by the entire organization. Chances are they will try and "scapegoat" someone in the process. Everyone puts on their Manager's hats and leaves the room, ready to justify the "decision" to the rest of the organization.

The pattern of Managers, Firefighters, and Exiles can be seen played out metaphorically in families, businesses, and societies. In the world scene, it is easy to tell at any given moment which country is playing what role. **The bottom line is people tend to set up their external reality to represent their internal reality**. Work, school, society, the world at large is arranged by silent agreement amongst members in this triad.

But the real irony is that as long as Managers run the world, society will be stuck in the Paradox. The problem is that there is no Self-leadership in the world. The true self is easy to recognize, a pleasure to deal with, and can do amazing things. Managers, on the other hand, are all about staying away from the Exiles while meeting the unmet emotional need at the same time.

The Paradox of the Manager and the Exile

Back for a moment to the metaphor of life as a garden. At about twenty, a man left home to start his own garden. He tilled, he weeded, and things did not grow the way he had anticipated. He tilled harder and longer. He watered more. He fertilized. He became a more persistent gardener. He tried meditation, affirmations, and goal setting. He played by the rules. He expected that cause and effect would work or that God would help him. Still the garden was barren. Something was terribly wrong.

This relates metaphorically to a child's experience of "being accepted" for who they are. Other examples could be being loved, feeling important, feeling secure, and so forth. It is important to note that in the beginning the child's definition of acceptance may be very narrow. During the attachment phase, this could take the form of the vague impression that, "If I cry and mommy comes, I am acceptable." As stated before, the brain looks for patterns and generalizes. What started as proximity seeking has been generalized to include affection. This in turn is generalized to include acceptance.

If acceptance is not experienced, a feeling of "unacceptability" becomes a type of habitual tendency in the brain. The Exile is constantly scanning for "unacceptability." By the time this person is an adolescent, "not being accepted" may have been generalized into poor performance at tasks or incompetence. "Nothing I do, no matter how spectacular, will ever please my parents." The young child is disowning and splitting. This split off *part* is the Exile. A child is vulnerable and will do anything to survive including sacrifice certain needs in order to please parents.

Children are demanding and needy. They need above all to be recognized as present and unique. They need to be accepted as they are. They need to have their pain and disappointment validated. If these things do not happen, the child learns to put on a brave managerial face, exile their pain, and banish their firefighting anger because of the pain. They may even ridicule other children who appear as needy in order to please their parents.

As a result, this particular person in the above example has an Exile with an unmet need for acceptance. It could just as well be a feeling of being unlovable, fear of abandonment, or any number of other fears. In the example of needing acceptance, the pain of not being accepted creates the Exile. The Exile holds this unmet need as the *part* that felt the disapproval. Unless there is trauma, this splitting may be a continuum of the attachment process and will be an outgrowth of the family system. The emotional burdening of this *part* could take years.

At the same time, the Manager is taking form. This is the *part* that finds acceptable ways of being in the world, "looking good," being disingenuous in order to get the unmet need fulfilled. In other words, the Exile holds the pain of the process of being invalidated and not receiving acceptance as a true self. The Manager then takes on the task of getting the needed acceptance through being a persona the world can accept.

This Manager is generalizing its role as well. "Daddy is a doctor. Therefore, if I become a Doctor when I grow up, he will accept me. Then I'll never have to feel the pain of the Exile!"

Some other examples of this Manager/Exile pairing include the "Workalcholic" trying desperately to gain the acceptance the Exile never felt he or she had. There is the "Achiever" striving mightily to accomplish ever-greater deeds in the hope of obtaining the recognition the Exile never felt it had. There is the "Know-It-All" who is continually trying to out shine everyone else so that the admiration the Exile never got will finally shine.

Then there is the "Perfectionist" desperately trying to be ever so good and helpful in order to get the love they never felt they had so their Exile will be fulfilled. What about the "Caretaker" manager? The "caretaker" *part* will be a doormat, serve every need in order to get some attention since the Exile *part* of them feels so ignored and insignificant.

Managers focus on *becoming*. This *part* scans for methods of *becoming* acceptable. *Becoming* a doctor, *becoming* successful, *becoming* rich, *having* children, *building* houses, *creating* a career and so forth. Managers are only concerned with the destination. They are not interested in stopping to smell the roses along the way. All of which is good on some level. But consider the words of the famous Buddhist writer and teacher, Thich Nhat Hanh, who says, "Death is the final destination. Why are you in such a hurry to get there?"

The Exile scans for evidence that reinforces the pain, while the Manager is scanning for ways of becoming, striving, achieving, reaching, grabbing, crawling, in a desperate attempt to erase the pain and fulfill the original unmet emotional need. The Exile exists in a state of being — being in a world where they are unacceptable, being invisible, being unrecognized and carrying the pain or the fear of that unmet emotional need.

Therein lies The Paradox of Being Human! The Manager's *striving* will never change a state of *being*. **Achieving does not equal having. The journey does not guarantee arrival**. The Manager tries. The fulfillment of unmet needs does not come from trying. As long as one continues to try, as long as they continue to strive, as long as they continue the effort to achieve, they can never *have*, *possess*, or *appropriate*.

A metaphor for this would be a woman holding onto a rock with her hands as tightly as she can. This is her Manager's striving. If someone tries to hand her a loaf of bread, she cannot take it without "letting go" of the rock (striving.) Therefore, as long as her Manager runs her life, she can never fulfill the need of the Exile. *Doing* does not fix *being*.

Let me just clarify the meaning here. Hard work is fine. Striving, for a time, is often appropriate. It's when one's efforts cross one's own boundaries of what is appropriate that they have entered into the pathology of an out of balance life that is all about hidden shame or fear. The Self suffers when this happens. The parts go to war with one another. Each person strives inside as well as outside. Life has no boundaries and there are no limits to hold a person back from a headlong plunge as he or she pretends there is true justification for their excessive *doingness*.

In the case of the example of needing acceptance, the Exile will feel the pain of being unacceptable. This part will scan the world for confirmation that, "Yes, I am unacceptable." Unacceptability is the fuel for the engine in this person's life. Meanwhile, the Manager has taken up the task of getting acceptance through striving, achieving, or being passive and making halfhearted attempts at success. The Manager, one's engine, will keep striving, scanning the world to strive more and strive more effectively. This becomes a lifestyle. **While**

the Exile sees a world of non-acceptance, the Manager is obsessed with manipulating the world to get acceptance.

In this particular example, "getting acceptance" becomes a life goal. It becomes thematic, a life theme. **Here is a person whose life theme is not having acceptance through striving for acceptance**. The paradox is that neither the Manager nor the Exile is equipped to perceive or acquire acceptance. The Exile perceives not having it and the Manager perceives striving for it. The failure of the Manager to get acceptance only reinforces the pain of the Exile's experience of not having it. The Exile, because of its pain, will not see the possibility of emotional fulfillment, while the Manager continues to strive to fulfill those unmet needs in order to avoid the Exile's pain. The life goal and lifestyle are essentially self-contradictory.

There is nothing wrong with wanting acceptance, recognition, love, security, or whatever one's unmet emotional need is. Each is a certainly valid premise for a life goal. It appears, however, humans think they must have a lifestyle of *striving* for it. That is a logical deduction. But in order to keep the cycle going, a person must constantly see themselves as not having what they want. If they didn't have this view of self-in-relationship to the world, the Manager would stop striving and the Exile would escape! The paradox is that no one can have acceptance in the active striving for it. No one can receive it if they cannot allow themselves to recognize it. They are in a double bind. They must strive to get it, but striving insures that their efforts will never end.

Be Spontaneous!

This is what Gerald Weeks and Luciano L'Abate call a "pragmatic paradox" in their book, *Paradoxical Psychotherapy*. Another term for this is a "double bind." The injunction "be spontaneous" is paradoxical. By definition as soon as one tries, they are no longer spontaneous. In order to obey it, they must disobey it.

In order to explain this, Weeks and L'Abate examine a *pathogenic double bind*. It is most interesting how these double blinds work in families and affect Exiles, Firefighters and Managers in setting up the Paradox.

The first requirement is be two or more persons who are closely connected. Certainly, this would apply to Exiles and Managers, and it applies to parent and child.

Secondly, there must be communication around a recurrent theme. Bingo! There is that word theme again. The theme in this case is not having acceptance or being unacceptable. A single occurrence does not make a theme. There must be a recurrent theme or burdening.

Thirdly, a primary negative injunction must occur. Weeks and L'Abate state that these take one of two forms: a) "Do so and so or I will punish you," or b) "If you do not do so in so, I will punish you." They say the learning context is one of avoidance of punishment.

What injunction could be communicated to a child to set up a pathogenic double bind? What happens if mom or dad constantly and repeatedly in word or deed in effect say, "If you're the kind of person you are, I can't accept you?" Or what about this, "If you don't act like someone other than who you are, I will not accept you?"

The fourth condition is that there must be a secondary injunction, either verbal or nonverbal, which conflicts with the first. For example "If you lie, you will be unacceptable?" Another example would be a mother telling a child, "If you are the kind of person you are, I can't accept you. And if you lie, you will be unacceptable as well."

Weeks and L'Abate state that a final negative injunction is communicated that prohibits the victim of the double bind from leaving the family or commenting on the untenable situation. The double bind, if it could be verbalized, becomes something like, "If you are who you are, you'll be punished. Furthermore, if you do not act like who you are not, you will be punished. We will deny that we know the real you, and if you tell the secret of our denial, you will be punished."

The person who does not want to feel the pain of being unacceptable is in a double bind. Therefore, he or she will attempt to structure a reality that supports that they are indeed unacceptable. However, the part that acts like someone else works very hard to be acceptable by acting out who they are not! This is called being stuck in the paradox.

The real paradox of lifestyle is that people will strive for acceptance, or love, or recognition, or whatever, but will never have it since having it would mean they could no longer strive for it. Of course, their failure to achieve it further fuels and confirms the pain of the Exile. This stimulates the Manager to strive even harder with the same negative results. It is a vicious cycle, a merry-go-round. At mid-life, no one has the energy to do it anymore.

In the Paradox of Being Human, value judgments set up an interior system that will never let a person off this merry-go-round. No one can *have* what he or she needs by *trying* to get it. *What is needed is the ability to see outside the box. Once one gets outside "the box" of their own system of parts they will see the effects of being stuck in paradox.* This is best summed up by the words of famous therapist and author Paul Watzlawick who wrote, "The situation is hopeless, but not serious!"

Chapter Ten

Persistence and Change

Now that we know of our plight with our *parts*, its time to do something about it. It is time to change, to get them into a healthy state so that we are not constantly acting out or pretending to be someone we're not. Fortunately, we have inside our head a built-in mechanism that can operate on our internal system of *parts* and produce dramatic change. That part of the brain is the Neo-Cortex, specifically the Frontal Lobes. In order to understand the power of the Frontal Lobes to produce dramatic change in our lives, we must first understand change itself. The Limbic System has its brand of change and the Frontal Lobes have their own radically different brand of change.

By now, most of us have seen the thought problem involving nine dots. The dots are arranged in the form of a square. The idea is to connect all of the dots by four straight lines without lifting the pen from the paper.

* * *

* * *

* * *

Almost everyone believes the lines must fall somewhere inside of the box. Of course, this is the assumption that makes solving the problem impossible. The solution to the problem involves "thinking outside of the box."

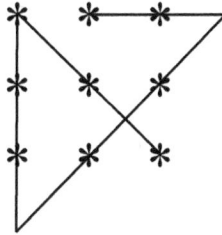

The problem is easily solved once you can "think outside of the box." (Manager *parts* love this stuff. Now companies hiring a new executive are looking for someone who can think outside the box).

A good example of this happened in 1334. The Duchess of Tyrol had encircled the castle of Hochosterwitz with her army. The castle was perched on a very steep rock rising high above the floor of the surrounding valley. A direct attack was impossible. The castle was impregnable. The only way to win a victory was to lay siege. This took time as her troops sealed the castle from outside supplies and waited. As time went on inside the castle, things began to deteriorate. Gradually they went through their stores and their condition became critical.

The Duchess had problems of her own about which the Commandant of the castle could not have known. Over time, her troops lost patience and became unmanageable. There was no end in sight to the siege, and she had urgent military problems elsewhere.

At the last moment in a desperate move, the Commandant ordered the last oxen slaughtered. He had the abdominal cavity filled with the remaining grain from stores. He then had the carcass thrown over the wall, down the cliff to the valley below. Upon seeing this, the Duchess, perceiving erroneously that the castle had plenty of food, abandoned the siege and moved her army from the area.

Meta

This is an example of going outside the box, or what is called second-order change. First-order change involves solving the problem from within the system of the problem. Second-order change involves getting outside of the problem system. The second order is a level above the problem, a meta-level. "Meta-" meaning a higher state.

But we all know how to change things, right? If at first you don't succeed, you try and try again. Then if that doesn't succeed, you try even harder. Still not succeeding? Try beating yourself up. How about a little self-ridicule? Still not working? Try, try again and again and again and again, repeatedly. Don't stop until you drop! This is what we humans do. We persistently do what does not work and then ask why it is not working. The next step is to blame God.

Persistence is called first-order change. That is change within the system of the problem. *More of the same* or persistence is supposed to solve the problem and create change. If you are driving on a hot day and you are uncomfortable, you turn on the AC. Still hot, turn on more air conditioning. More of the same works, doesn't it?

In the book, *Change*, the authors, Paul Watzlawick, John Weakland, and Richard Fisch, use the example of alcoholism. Obviously, alcohol is a problem with many ramifications. When drinking is a problem, restrictions must be put on consumption. When that didn't work in this country, we outlawed the consumption of alcohol. Prohibition brought with it problems far more enormous than the original problem of drinking. In other words, the solution became the problem.

Another example where the attempted solution becomes the problem is sleeplessness. You have trouble falling asleep, so you try harder. You count sheep, try to clear your mind. The harder you try; the harder it becomes. It is well known that in order to fall asleep, one must not be thinking about going to sleep. Falling asleep is a spontaneous process, not one of intention.

Take the following situation: You are married to someone who is an introvert who does not readily converse with you. This makes you uncomfortable since you need that verbal connection in order to feel complete in the relationship. You attempt repeatedly to engage your spouse in conversation. Sometimes all you get is a grunt. Sometimes you get no response at all. Maybe they did not hear you. Try a little louder. They get uncomfortable and shift in the chair, but still you are not getting the response you want. For now, you give up in resentment. The next day you try again. You have several things on your mind and you want to talk. Your partner sits in silence. You are not sure he/she even heard you. "Did you hear me?" Finally, you are hollering at the top of your voice. "Did you hear me?" "Yeah, Yeah, Yeah." They assume a more closed body position. The next day you are more determined than ever to communicate. As soon as you see him/her, you leap. You complain that they never listen that they don't care about you. You cry, demand; raise your voice, whimper. Finally, they roll their eyes and leave the room.

This is an example of how more of the same does not work. Persistently doing what does not work eventually causes the attempted solution to become the problem! Persistence is an example of first-order change, or change from within the system of the problem.

Ironically, the fastest way to create communication in the above example would be to do exactly the opposite as common sense would tell us. In other words, leave your mate alone. Give them all the space they need. Get busy doing other things. Oh, and by the way, this must be done without resentment and without sending a lot of pouting nonverbal messages of displeasure. Eventually, they will come around and say, "Hey, what's going on? You are so quiet. Is there something you'd like to talk about?" This is second-order change or change from a level higher than the system of problem formation.

In life, we can see many instances of first-order change where the attempted solution becomes the problem. Dieting is an example. This certainly is an example where persistence pays off, right? Wrong! When one diets, a part inside may feel deprived waiting for the day when the diet is over to begin binge eating again. It's a proven fact that dieting burns up muscle tissue and lowers metabolic rate making it less likely that the diet will be a long term solution.

Those who have been successful have changed their relationship to the problem or *reframed* the problem. They have focused on ways of improving their health, self-image, and strength without worrying about food directly. Oprah trained for a marathon. Many people take up low fat cooking as a hobby. Some combine exercise into a long-term lifestyle change. The cycle of eating, gaining weight, feeling lousy, going on a diet, and going back to eating is a solution that sets up its own problem system.

Susan Powter's book, *Stop the Insanity* is an effort to look at the weight loss system from a second-order level. She talks about how the attempted solution to the problem becomes the problem. The subtitle says, "Eat, Breathe, Move." These are not the themes of first-order change. They are second-order injunctions that have nothing to do with the standard dieting paradigm. More importantly, I see something fascinating on the cover of this book. There is not one, but two pictures of Susan Powter with her head nearly shaved!

It is a statement that she is no longer willing to be part of the problem system of overweight, self-hatred, and living up to everyone else's image of what looks good. This is an outside example of interior change. She reoriented herself and her life to "stop the insanity." Cutting her hair, for her, was part of that second-order change.

Second-Order Change

During the nineteenth-century, there were many riots in Paris. The commander of an army detachment received orders one day to clear the City Square by shooting the rabble. The commander ordered his men to take up firing positions and then addressed the crowd. "Mesdames, m'sieurs, I have orders to fire at the rabble. But as I see a great number of honest, respectable citizens before me, I request that they leave so that I can safely shoot the rabble." The square was empty within a few minutes.

First-order change nearly always involves what is reasonable or logical.

However, persistence at the first-order level merely reinforces the problem system and causes the attempted solution to become the problem.

Second-order change seems always to involve decisive action not on the problem but on **the attempted solution** to the problem. Watzlawick and his co-authors discovered four principles about second-order change:

1. Second-order change is applied to what appears to be the solution at the first-order level. At the second-order level, the "solution" reveals itself as what is maintaining the problem. For instance, "trying harder" is a first order solution. At the next logical level, it is easy to see that persistently doing what is not working in fact maintains the problem.

2. While first-order change always appears to be based on common sense, second-order change appears weird, unexpected, puzzling, and paradoxical.

3. Applying second-order change techniques to the "solution" means that the situation is dealt with in the here and now. These techniques deal with the effects, not the presumed causes; the crucial question is *what* and not *why*. In other words, the problem is not your behavior; it's my emotional reaction to your behavior. This is far different from saying, "you make me mad." Alternatively, "I wouldn't get angry if you would behave differently." Both of these statements lay blame for problem feelings at the other person's feet. Second order change requires me to take responsibility for my emotional reactions exclusive of what's going on around me. Therefore, I am opening space for other people to change their behavior.

4. Second-order change techniques lift the situation out of the self-reflexiveness of paradox-engendered traps by reframing the entire problem. A good example of this was presented earlier where one person nags their partner in an attempt to get him to come closer. Instead, he moves further away to get away from the nagging. When he does this, she nags even more persistently. His efforts are therefore paradoxical in that the result of his efforts at solving the problem reinforce the problem system and therefore make it self-reflexive or turning back on itself.

When we take full responsibility for our emotional reactions we are in effect saying, "I am feeling shame or fear when you behave in a certain way. I am not asking you to change your behavior; I am asking you to help me with my feelings. You therefore are free to behave in any way you want to behave, but I must fulfill my unmet emotional needs and take care of my feelings in a way that is appropriate for me. In other words, I am accepting you rather than asking you to change."

When a couple comes in for therapy there is typically so much anger, fire fighting, and defending that it's hard to see the shame and the fear. When one partner finally realizes that the other's *Exile* is terrified of abandonment and that she is defending, he can see the nagging, pursuing, and begging for what it is – a desperate attempt for an emotional connection. With this insight, it becomes easier for him to give a nurturing response rather than moving away. As you might imagine this does not happen immediately. Getting people out of their firefighting mode is reasonably difficult. But once they are tired of fighting they are willing to look at process as opposed to the content. That's when compassion helps bring healing. I help couples reach this state by teaching how to move away from first order attempts at changing their partner's behavior and instead look deeply inside of themselves and confessing their true feelings. This new frame of reference produces second order change.

Milton Erickson Revisited

No one understood change better than Milton Erickson did. One client, an older man, came to Erickson with a problem of chronic insomnia. In order to fall asleep each night he had resorted to using a drug. Usually the first dose would not work, so after a fitful period he would take more and then sleep only about an hour at a time. The man lived with his son, and during the conversation, Erickson learned that the house had hardwood floors that needed waxing. The old man had quite an aversion to the smell of the stuff.

We have talked about the injunction, "be spontaneous" concerning sleep. The man was caught in one of those loops of trying to solve a problem where the *trying* itself had become the problem. Erickson could have prescribed relaxation or any number of first-order solutions.

Instead, he did something totally unexpected. He told the man that he could cure him, but he would have to follow Erickson's instructions precisely. The instructions were to spend four nights waxing the floors. The patient said he would try anything. By the fourth night, he was so exhausted he lay down and said, "If I don't fall asleep in fifteen minutes, I've got to polish the floors all night, and I mean it too!" It turned out the man was willing to do anything to avoid waxing the floors, even falling asleep.

Many have dubbed this method the ordeal technique! By creating an ordeal, waxing the floors, the original problem was no longer viewed at the first order level. Erickson had reframed it so that the symptom, sleeplessness, was juxtaposed against an ordeal. This meant that the old man had to view the problem from a meta-level, a different perspective. This story is also a good example of how the ordeal is also tied to the attempted solution, *trying*. Trying to fall asleep is now no longer an attempted solution. The attempted solution is now related to the ordeal! At this new level of viewing the problem, the only alternative left vis-à-vis the ordeal is to give up the solution - *trying*. Giving up, therefore, leads directly to sleep.

There have literally been volumes written about Erickson and his work. So bizarre are his case histories that writers have devoted thousands of pages trying to quantify his "techniques." However, the very fact that his methods were so unorthodox tells us that he was moving to a meta-level in dealing with therapeutic problems. That is how second order change looks, weird, spontaneous and unexpected. We will see later that moving to a meta-level by definition means that the problem can no longer be a problem. The attempted solution is the problem when viewed at the next highest level. Persistent attempts at first-order change maintain problems making them loom ever larger in our lives. In order to keep a problem; we must persistently do what is not working. In order to make the problem worse; we must try to solve it with more determination. In order to solve the problem we must move into the meta-self.

Parts, Persistence and Polarization

Continued attempts at first-order change are what keep our internal *parts* polarized and extreme. Emotional reactivity is an attempt at change on the first-order level. In my case, I have a disowned *part* or an Exile that is weak and vulnerable. I also have a managerial *part* that is strong and confident. This is polarization. The feelings of the Exile will cause a corresponding shoring up of the strength of the Manager. Each *part* in turn reacts to the response of the other. Both become more and more extreme in the way they represent themselves. This increasing extreme behavior is an attempt to change the system at the first-order level.

I was so polarized in this way, that even after my work with *parts*, I still have an interesting problem. When I want to talk about my feelings to my partner, I sound like a radio announcer. The more vehement I think I am being, the more my voice tone and affect convey that it's no big deal and I can handle it. It is a strange sensation to know that internal change is happening and that the polarizations are no longer there in the same way only to discover that my internal experience *is still not congruent* with what I convey to those around me.

This has forced me to monitor how my message is being received. In other words, to be conscious. I have to make an effort to say, although I may not sound like it, I have deep feelings that I want to share. My partner then has to concentrate on listening. First, she must really "hear" me and secondly she must insure that my Manager *part* is not activating a Manager *part* in her that wants to believe I am really talking about the weather. Her Manager has a personal stake in not identifying with my feelings. If that were to happen, her Exiles might be activated.

Both Richard Schwartz and Paul Watzlawick use the example of sailors on a sailboat to exemplify problem formation and polarization. When a sailboat is leaned over by the wind everyone on board has to move to the other side in order to steady the boat. Imagine two sailors doing the same thing, one leaning out over one side and the other leaning out over the other side. Should one sailor lean further out, the other must do so as well to keep the boat upright. Neither sailor can safely move back toward the middle of the boat for fear of tipping it over.

These sailors represent the extreme nature of internal *parts*. If one *part* becomes a little more extreme, the polarized *part*, the one on the opposite side of the boat, must become more extreme to compensate. Most people want to get rid of the extreme behaviors of the Firefighters. Without understanding the polarization and seeing the other extreme *part* on the other side of the boat, change is hopeless. As life goes on, the Exiles scream ever louder since they are exiled and our primary Manager does not want to listen to them either. In response, the Firefighters become more extreme in their behavior to defend against those feelings. Both are attempts at first-order change. Clearly, this polarization not only forms problems early in life, but also maintains problems throughout life.

Usually, at midlife we wake up to the fact that this is not working. Unless we have access to second-order change to rebalance the system, we will become more "shut down," unaware and uni-dimensional.

I once sat next to an older gentleman on an airplane. He was tall, slim, and wore jeans. There was something about his carriage that spoke of wealth and success. It turned out that he was the 79-year-old former Chairman of the Board of a Fortune 100 company. When I learned this, I remembered seeing him on the cover of a national business magazine.

He spent the entire time talking about business. He had retired and started another business after years of life at the very top of the corporate ladder. He said that at his age he felt vibrant, alive, and excited about his new venture. This man may or may not have been worth hundreds of millions of dollars, but I am quite sure from our chat that he was worth tens of millions. As we talked, it became readily apparent that he had a Manager *part* that was frantic to stay "busy." He was obsessed with business, success, and the game of it all.

Then he made a comment that shocked me! Just before the plane landed, he turned to me and said, "Work is good, isn't it? It keeps you away from the sadness!" His comment was completely out of context and I was taken aback. But what a revealing thing to say. His comment served to put me in touch with his sadness. I could not imagine what his personal losses had been along the way or where his sadness came from. I also did not know exactly how much of himself he had had to amputate in order to keep up the race away from that sadness and toward the boardroom. But it was lamentable to see a gentleman so charismatic, intelligent and vital whose only experience of life after all his success was that of one *part* "working" hard so he didn't have to deal with that other *part* lurking in the background ready to flood him with unwanted feelings.

That is not to say that he should not have been working. However, as we shall see, internal balance, harmony, and leadership allow us to be fully alive and to enjoy the full experience of life. We learn that we need not run away from pain at all. Once you turn to face it, it transforms. There is fear that once one acknowledges the Exiles, their pain will be overwhelming and flood the person for the rest of their life. As it turns out, this is not the case. Through self-leadership, we can calm the Exiles and the Firefighters, thereby changing the way they represent themselves in our lives.

It seems counterintuitive, but ignoring the pain, ridiculing the acting out, and scoffing at our selves only intensifies all the stuff we'd rather see go away. Acknowledgement, tolerance, and understanding are the attitudes of the true self. I call this the Meta-Self. It is the focal point, the doorway into the full enjoyment of our lives and loved ones. It is the state, which changes our experience of the universe.

Chapter Eleven

The Meta-Self

One day a student asked P.D. Ouspensky, the Russian teacher and mathematician, "I understand that we have to create our own 'I' out of nothing. What creates 'I'?" Ouspensky's answer explains something about *parts* and one's own brain.

"First, self-knowledge. There is a very good Eastern allegory that deals with the creation of 'I'. Man is compared to a house full of servants, without master or steward to look after them. So the servants do whatever they like; none of them does his own work. The house is in a state of complete chaos, because all the servants try to do someone else's work which they are not competent to do. The cook works in the stables, the coachman in the kitchen, and so on. The only possibility for things to improve is if a certain number of servants decide to elect one of themselves as a deputy steward and in this way make him control the other servants. He can do only one thing: he puts each servant where he belongs and so they begin to do their right work. When this is done, there is the possibility of the real steward coming to replace the deputy steward and to prepare the house for the master. We do not know what the real steward means or what the master means, but we can take it that the house is full of servants and the possibility of a deputy steward

describes our situation. This allegory helps us understand the beginning
of the possibility of creating a permanent 'I'."

To understand what Ouspensky is saying, a person could imagine himself
or herself walking through a meadow in the foothills of soaring mountains.
There are snowcaps on the mountains, but it is a warm day with just a touch
of crispness to the clean mountain air. The sun is high in the sky and off to the
east they can see a few puffy clouds in an otherwise cloudless vista. They stay
with this experience for just a few moments.

Now, for a moment, they pull back to a position somewhat above this
tranquil scene. From this vantage point above, they can watch themselves
below. They might notice how they are walking. They could see the details of
their pace or gait. They could even see the hair on the top of their head. They
might notice how the sunlight reflects and highlights the color. They could
see how far they have walked, and what direction they are going. They might
have a perspective on how much further they could walk before turning back
toward home.

This little exercise was simple. Nevertheless, they did set up an interior
scene and they placed an *analog* or a version of themselves in a meadow in their
mind's eye. The next thing they did was to assume the position above to watch
the self below. This perspective allowed them to become an observer of the
analog "I." Psychologist and author Julian Jaynes has labeled the "you" above
who observes as the metaphor "me." In his book, *The Origin of Consciousness
in the Break-Down of the Bicameral Mind*, he says, "Conscious mind is a spatial
analog of the world and mental acts are analogs of bodily acts." What this means
is that in order to be self-aware one must first create a space inside of one's head
and then observe a representation of one's own behavior.

Jaynes says," We have said that consciousness is an operation rather than
a thing, a repository, or a function. It operates by way of analogy, by way of
constructing an analog space with an analog 'I' that can observe that space,
and move metaphorically in it."

The ability to perform self-observation and self-referencing is a function of the
frontal lobes of the neocortex. The chapter discussing metaphors referred to this as
self-in-relation-to-self - one of the metaphorms. Self-awareness or consciousness
means one is aware of their *process* of being as opposed to the *content* of being.

The analog "I" is obsessed with *content,* or what is perceived to be happening.
The analog "I" is one's awareness of one's self having an experience. A person
is in his or her body seeing what they see, hearing what they hear. They are
fully associated with the experience. They know they are in their analog "I"
when they need to be right, when they make a value judgment, when they tell
their story and try to prove their point. The analog "I" will give a first person
account as if re-experiencing the event.

The analog "I" is another way of saying *parts*. A person is living as a
reactive part when he or she is "in" the experience and they tell the story

about the experience. Parts are in the first person; I said this, I did that. The analog "I" is completely addicted to drama -- the soap opera quality of life, the sensations, and the feelings.

The metaphor "me" is something quite different. One knows they are in a self-observing "me" when they say something like, "When I hear you say that, I feel afraid that you don't care about me. I also notice I feel somewhat defensive." The self-observer makes process-oriented comments not content-oriented comments. "As I observed myself walking through the meadow below, I noticed that I bent down to pick a flower." This is a process comment. A content comment might be, "my visualization was beautiful." Notice that content immediately calls for a value judgment. Self-awareness then is a metaphor "me" watching an analog "I" from an outside perspective.

I once had a client who had been to an appointment related to seeking employment. As the meeting progressed, she became increasingly impatient and upset. This was a description of how her parts were being activated. She noticed her reactivity and realized in a flash what she was experiencing. Because of this perspective, she said to herself, "Say, I've got a bad attitude here!"

This may seem like a subtle shift, but it's actually a huge change. To go from *content* to *process* in this case means that she had to move from her reactivity to observing her reactivity, from the analog "I" to the metaphor "me." In other words, she shifted from having an experience to observing herself in the process of having it.

By shifting from *content* to *process*, she now has the choice of how to act in the situation. She will see new and more powerful choices she can make. If she had stayed reactive, she no doubt would have found a way to communicate her displeasure, which would have had a direct effect on the outcome of the situation. **When she began observing her process, she immediately had choices as to how to take care for self.**

Ouspensky said, "One will never get self-consciousness so long as one believes that one has it."

What this means is that self-consciousness or self-awareness is an active process. When a person stops the active process of observing himself or herself, they are no longer conscious and are merely acting as if they have awareness. That happens when a person assumes that he or she is aware without making the effort to be aware. Therefore, self-consciousness or self-awareness is an active state of mind, not something to be achieved and then forgotten.

I have had many clients who have looked me right in the eye and said, "I have already dealt with that." This is interesting. It is an example of someone who has done some growth work and now assumes that they don't need to look at that anymore. The problem is that each person needs to deal with individual issues on a moment-by-moment basis. Self-awareness is the act of watching one's parts. This is what Ouspensky means when he says "remembering ourselves."

Evidence of the Meta-Self

The notion of self-awareness or self-observation relates directly back to neurology. It turns out that brain research supports this view of a metaphor "me." Antonio Damasio, the author of *Decarte's Error*, sees a self-observing function at work in the brain.

In an earlier chapter, the example was used of remembering the image of a friend. When the image of a friend is seen the observer responds through the action of habitual tendencies in the brain. Just like having a rock thrown in a pool of water, the observer is in a particular state of being and then the friend appears. The result is two states of self interacting with one another like ripples on a pond. It is an interference pattern. This is what Damasio referred to as the "self perturbed," or the experience of the *self* in the process of changing. This is like the laser light example of the beam splitter and the interference pattern. That's what a "perturbation" is, an interference pattern. This "change state" or interference pattern is what the brain records as the observer's perceived present experience.

Although this experience is "real," the *self* that is actually experiencing the experience cannot "know" or be self-observing since it is an analog "I." It can only experience and then respond to that experience. Damasio states, "Although the responding process implies knowledge, it's certainly does not imply that any brain component 'knows' that responses are being generated to the presence of an entity. When the organism's brain generates a set of responses to an entity, the existence of the representation of self does not make the self know that its corresponding organism is responding."

What Damasio is saying is that the *self* that is having the experience cannot, at the same time, observe itself having the experience. In other words, the self-state can participate in content; can tell an autobiographical story, i.e. the analog "I." But this is not process-oriented. The *self* has no self-awareness. This is exactly our experience of *parts*. *Parts* are analogs and therefore cannot experience awareness of themselves. All they can do is experience and then react to that experience.

To solve the problem of self-awareness or "knowing," Damasio postulates a third set of neural nets that is outside the experience of seeing and responding to the friend's image. This "third party ensemble" receives signals from the objective world; in this case, it would be sensory images of the friend. It also receives the changing self-state or this person's reaction to their internal experience of seeing their friend. Much of this information is generated automatically by the Limbic System. Using these two inputs, this third party network can build an internal representation of the *self* in the process of changing - in other words self-observation. This is why I say *process* as opposed *content*. Damasio calls this third party network the Meta-*Self*. Meta-because it is one level above the level of the experience itself. *Self* because it is the metaphor "me" or the one inside who observes.

Damasio sums this up by saying, "I propose that subjectivity emerges during the latter step when the brain is producing not just images of an object, not just images of organism responses to the object, but a third kind of image, that of an organism in the act of perceiving and responding to an object." The implications of this are profound given the principles of second order change discussed earlier. What this means is that problem systems are maintained at the *self*-level of the experience or the analog "I." Problems at this level are maintained and reinforced through persistence or more of the same. However, humans have a built-in neurological platform for second-order change: the Meta-*Self*. At this level, an individual has the ability to observe the process of *parts* activation and problem maintenance and to comment about it. This is what distinguishes humans from animals.

When I throw a plastic ball on the floor, my cat, Dusty will chase it, bat it, and play with it until he's exhausted. If he could talk, he would say, "Let's do it again, let's do it again!" However, he could not say, "You know, I crack myself up. When you throw that ball, I feel compelled to chase it and play with it. Hell, I'm even aware it's not really alive. But I have a whale of a time with it, nevertheless." He could only say that if he had frontal lobes, which he does not.

The Process of Change

Two people are having an argument. The very fact that they are arguing indicates that they already have a *part* in each of them activated. They are arguing, and they both want to win the argument. What strategies could they use to win? Well, one could try arguing louder. Possibly, at that point the other might argue in a more "adult" tone of voice, which is designed to infuriate the first person since the second adult's tone mocks their teenage shouting. Okay, one must take a different tack - become more intellectual and logical. "If, then, thusly, therefore, and in summary!" Virginia Satir called this "super-reasonableness."

The other might then become strategic or perhaps decide to bring up all the similar arguments the two may have had in the past. One could generalize using words like "always" or "never." Perhaps the other could use an affective technique to throw the first person off, like a single tear sliding down their face. It is hard to attack a victim.

The point is that all of these are first-order attempts at ending the argument. However, as can be seen, persistently trying to win the argument only raises the stakes to argue more, more loudly, vehemently, logically, whatever. How is the problem of arguing solved? The real problem is trying to win the argument. The attempted solution, winning, has become the problem.

What would happen if they both engaged their frontal lobes and started to comment on the *process* of arguing rather than the *content* of the argument? "I noticed that when you said that I needed to lose twenty pounds that I went inside and heard my mother say the same thing. I felt devalued when you said that. When she said it in years past, I always felt devalued."

"Well, that's interesting, because I noticed during our exchange that I wasn't really listening to you. I was having an internal dialogue in an extremely critical voice rehearsing what I was going to say next."

"I think I was doing the same thing. Only my critical voice sounds like *my* mother. You know, when I was yelling at you, I was repeating some of the same things she used to say to me."

As long as each is commenting on process, they can no longer argue. In fact, *parts* activation is not possible as long as we stay curious about the process that occurred and is occurring. Then if I say something that triggers a *part* of another person, they can say, "You know, I just had the urge to defend against what you just said. The funny thing is that I know you were commenting on your internal experience, but it must have pushed a button for me. I need to explore this feeling."

Again, staying process-oriented engages the Meta-*Self* and prevents the argument. These self-observations come from a meta-level above the argument. Commenting on the process of arguing is meta- to the argument itself. *One cannot argue and stay in a Meta-Self role.*

This is a simple example, but it dramatically demonstrates the value of the frontal lobes of the neo-cortex. Through self-observation and self-referencing, people cannot maintain problems that involve their reactivity. The Meta-*Self* is a built-in neurological platform for second-order change. From this platform, they can observe the actions of their parts. They can see polarization, imbalance, and those results in their lives. It is my contention that self-observation alone can change the internal system of *parts*. Let me say that another way. Self-observation changes the system. This does not mean that always and every time it solves all problems. Self-observation, when practiced, allows the system to be re-framed due to one's new perspective. This very act by definition will change the system. Sometimes this can create radical change all by itself.

Let me relay a story about one of my clients, Toni. Toni had been raised in a violent alcoholic family. Consequently, she was extremely fear-based. When she was around someone who was in a reaction, especially anger, she felt she needed to take care of it. She would step in and make all kinds of attempts to get the other person to calm down. After just a few short sessions of therapy, she met her Exile. Her Exile was an extremely frightened child, a young version of herself. She was able to separate herself from that part and from that moment on was able to manage her reactivity in a new and very resourceful way. Literally, from one session to the next, she realized that when her Exile was activated there was nothing for her to do anymore. From that moment on, she was nearly always able to exercise self-leadership and more choices even in a situation that before would have been perceived as dangerous. The insight about her Exile and where it came from meant she was able to use the awareness that "this reaction is about yesterday, today is today, and I don't need to do the same thing anymore because I don't live there anymore."

Sometimes these miraculous changes astonish even me, and I see them on a regular basis. Self-observation requires the individual to separate their frontal lobes from their Limbic System where the problem system is being maintained. This frees the individual to act. When one is in re-action, one cannot make appropriate choices. The question is one of right action. In other words, when I have a reaction what is the right action to take? Many people say they cannot deal with the situation or reaction until they calm down. Well, by then their primary Manager part has taken over, so that part can act!

Self-observation lets me see what is happening both inside and outside my mind. It lets me see external and internal reality. It lets me question, is my perception correct? Your Exile will always see/perceive things the same way whether they really are that way or not. When I question my perception, I notice I'm having a reaction, but I'm able to find out if this or that person intended to come across the way I am interpreting it.

Self-observation not only helps change our internal system of parts, it is also the doorway into perceiving what is really happening around me. *Parts* activation only allows a narrow, predefined set of inappropriate responses. Self-observation, on the other hand, allows me to check my internal tendencies with what is really going on around me and make new choices. Therefore, it is important to understand that the goal is not to get rid of reactivity. The goal is, through observation, to notice the reactivity and understand how that reaction relates to what is really going on. That is the only way that one can use self-preserving strategies for protection and to meet one's emotional needs.

As I say this, I realize that it all sounds so easy. It is not! In the next chapter, I will discuss what's necessary to establish the *self* as leader of the internal system. Often this is not an automatic process, and I do not mean to make light of its difficulty. Nevertheless, a fundamental understanding of the principles of internal change at the Meta-level is vital to having the initiative for second-order change. This means one cannot force it, will it, or beat one's self up over it. Each individual must, however, become a serious student of their own internal process so they can get their needs met. The Limbic System, with all its crying, yelling, and demanding, will never get the job done. People will never go free in the midst of all of their reactivity no matter how self-preserving their intent. It is only through freedom from reactivity and through self-leadership, that each can ask for and finally get what they want and need. Had I not gone through this process I would never be experiencing the fulfillment in life that I am today.

As one attempts to identify their parts, their reactivity and origins, it is important to understand what "process" means. Process is not the realization that a person has a low self-concept because of poor potty training, for example. Knowing the genesis of a part or the origin of the pattern may be helpful in understanding one's inappropriate reactions. Understanding that all the "damage" that one's parents did may be gratifying. However, this is not what process is about. It is the moment-by-moment awareness of how a person experiences the world. It is a person's noticing what happens inside as they constantly adjust to input in their lives. *It is about what is happening, not why*.

Autobiographical Me

One thing that has puzzled me for some time is the actual identity of *self* and *parts*. As we stated earlier, the description of a *part* is really a metaphor for the internal process. Nonetheless, that representation still can be a lever for change in the system. I have noticed that Exiles tend to be young children, Firefighters are nearly always teenagers, and Managers tend to be either parentified-children or adult-like in their descriptions.

This prompts questions about these *parts* and the *self* that people all have. Experts know that when young children are abused severely that they develop the ability to dissociate. They also know that these split off *parts* do not take on a separate identity, as in MPD until the time of life when identities are actually constructed. This time, according to John Kotre noted memory expert, is adolescence. In healthy people, adolescence is the time when identity is established. In sufferers of MPD, this is when alternate personalities emerge.

So, what is happening here? What about the Exiled child within? Does it date from childhood or is it a function of adult autobiographical memory? In Kotre's book, *White Gloves*, he explores the earliest memories of people. What he finds is that these early memories contain cognitive content that could not possibly have been developed by the time of the "memory." This does not mean the memory is false in the sense of the current ongoing debate. Often these memories contain elements of interpreting emotions, understanding adult language, meaning, and concepts. An actual early childhood memory (before the age of two or three) would be a mix of sounds, touch, taste and smell which would not always be distinct from one another. What Kotre found was that too many memories of the "child within" are from impossible visual perspectives. Many memories are anachronistic in some way. For example, a voice or eyes of later years are superimposed on those of a child. Often there is an understanding of language or stories that is too advanced.

Psychologist Allyssa McCabe and her colleagues found that few four year olds have the capability to create stories, which build to a climax and then resolve the plot. Adolescents, when asked to recount memories, tended to include perspectives that would not have been possible in early childhood. McCabe also showed that adult's narrative accounts of childhood incidents have a structure that comes from years later than the date of the "memory." Again, this does not mean the memory is false. It does mean that as one grows older and the brain develops greater abilities, which influences the way one recreates a memory.

Some of this came up in the discussion of *parts*. What does all of this have to do with *self*? Well, it depends on how "self" is defined. *The New American Heritage Dictionary*, defines self first as "The total, essential, or particular being of a person; the individual." This sounds like the whole ball of wax, the whole enchilada - each person, as a whole is a *self*. Next, this same dictionary gives this definition for *self*: "The essential qualities distinguishing one person from another; individuality . . ." Now it appears that self is further viewed not just as the whole person, but as that which makes one unique as an individual. Finally, there is a third definition; "One's consciousness of one's own being or identity . . ."

Research has shown that this ability to be self-conscious does not develop until adolescence and does not reach full maturity until the late teens. This does not mean however, that before this, children are not aware of their experiences. It is just that they do not have the ability to comment on or observed the *self* that is having the experience. Therefore, in a broad sense, *self* is an ever-changing somewhat nebulous internal representation that evolves as individual neural development becomes more sophisticated and he or she has more life experiences. In a personal sense, however, the "*self*" is not whole until a person is in junior high or high school. This is one reason that the teen years are so difficult and tumultuous. Each one is busy defining and discovering a *self*.

Even the ability to describe *parts* is developmental. Autobiographical memory develops such that one's metaphor for internal *parts* changes with age and one's ability to describe our internal experience is a function of a brain in the process of growing.

Some theorists have proffered the notion that the "self" can be shattered, destroyed, or damaged in early childhood. This runs counter to current findings about the brain. Since each person's ability to observe the self in the process of change (the interference pattern referred to earlier like a rock being thrown in a pond - one experience on top of another) doesn't fully develop until the teen years, it's hard to understand how the *self* could somehow be shattered or damaged in early childhood. In fact, if a person makes it through to early adulthood, they arrive fully equipped with a Neo-cortex ready to step forward to assume leadership over the Limbic System of *parts*. The problem is that by then the system of *parts* is so dominant that a person must be able to overcome the flooding, blending, and masquerading that hold the self hostage.

In other words, it appears that people have never been told that self-awareness, self-consciousness, self-reflection, or self-referencing has much of a purpose other than just some form of passive introspection. These are not action concepts. My assertion here is that the Meta-Self can take action, dramatic action. It is the only way to achieve lasting change, second-order change, of one's internal system.

Ouspensky put it this way:

> "Self-remembering is an attempt to be aware of yourself. Self-observation is always directed at some definite function: either you observe your thoughts, or movements, or emotions, or sensations. It must have a definite object that you observe in yourself. Self-remembering does not divide you, you must remember the whole, it is simply the feeling of 'I', of your own person."

The action each can take is to observe their *parts* in action, to notice their reactivity, and to see how much of their emotional content is appropriate for the current situation and how much is related to their personal history. Yet, one can do more. Once a person learns to observe, he or she can lead with the *self*. It is amazing what a place of power it is to be master of reactivity and stay present in a situation. The choices become endless and the outcomes miraculous.

Chapter Twelve

Self Rediscovered

Everything is now in place to take back our lives from the ravages of value judgments from outside of us. Before we do, let's summarize the key points that have been made so far to put the next task in perspective. First, the process of attachment was discussed. Because attachment is about survival for the infant and because attachment is so primal, our attachment style becomes an underlying driving force in our lives. This style becomes more sophisticated, complex, and generalized. One example of generalization happens when one assigns their current relationship the role that would have been played by their mother or father. One intimate relationship has been generalized to all intimate relationships. Our family system and the culture around us reinforce our attachment style. Pressures from within the system and from caregivers in the form of Original Sin or value judgments causes the splitting of *parts* that are disowned and pushed into the shadow.

Then a neurological basis for *parts* was established and for parallel processing in the brain. *Scanning, projection,* were discussed along with emotional reactivity and how it is set up in the Limbic System before the Neo-Cortex is fully developed. These parts organize themselves into the three roles they play in the internal family system: Exiles, Firefighters, and Managers. This set the stage for unveiling The Paradox of Being Human, and how the reflexive interplay of the Exiles and Managers keeps us on a never-ending treadmill of effort resulting in continued dissatisfaction.

Next, there was another brain function. The frontal lobes of the Neo-Cortex give us a Meta-Self. Through an understanding of the principles of first and second-order change, the meta-perspective of the frontal lobes was presented as well as how, through self-awareness and self-observation, each one has a built-in platform for second-order change in their lives. Now that the Meta-Self has been revealed, let's see how to establish that self in the role of leader in our lives.

A Sense of Self

Given internal imbalance, polarization, and disharmony, the need for a leader becomes clear. The problem is, for most of us, the leader is really a Manager or some other *part*. In Schwartz's IFS (Internal Family Systems) model, none of the *parts* can be the leader. For one thing, they are all extreme in their viewpoints and behaviors. For another, each *part* only has one behavioral choice, which results from its distorted viewpoint. Moreover, since the *parts* are frozen in time and not really in the present, this single choice is nearly always inappropriate!

As was explained in the last chapter, the *self* is an undeveloped piece of our interior world. The *parts* know this and can easily bump it out of the way when they want to. Reflecting back to my own personal moment of enlightenment, one of the things I experienced when I suddenly became free of all of my baggage was a *self* that was fully and completely differentiated from my *parts*. It was as if that "still small voice" finally could speak up.

This is what Core Transformation calls the "core self." When the *self* stands alone, life becomes a vivid and powerful experience. When this happened, I was experienced an overwhelming peace and a confidence I had never fully felt.

In his book, *The Power of Myth*, Joseph Campbell says, "If you do follow your bliss, you put yourself on a kind of track that has been there all the while, waiting for you, and the life that you ought to be living is the one you are living. Wherever you are - if you are following your bliss, you are enjoying that refreshment, that life within you, all the time."

Isn't this the essence of the experience of *self*? When I read it, I was struck by how precisely Campbell had explained what I had discovered through my transformational experience. Were it not for value judgments, a person would have the full time experience of this as their birthright.

However, as I pointed our earlier, our sense of *self* is defined as self-in-relationship. Leadership is how we organize ourselves in relation to our *parts*. We should not assume that the Meta-Self merely stands and observes. Recently, I have heard a new homily from some of my new age friends. "We must become parents to our inner child." And that in short is what the *self* must do. The *self* must learn to acknowledge all *parts*. It may be necessary to soothe a frightened *part* or calm an angry *part*. The *self* must take an active, even parental role, with the *parts*. By parental, I do not mean critical. Good parenting comes from guidance with a firm, but loving, hand. This is also a good definition of leadership.

Trauma and Abuse

Gwen had been referred to me by one my colleagues. The first time I met her she sat in the chair opposite me ringing her hands and furtively looking around the room. At first, I thought she might be shy, and that it would take many weeks before the details of her life came forward. This was not the case. Within minutes, she was telling me of the incest she had survived as a young child. By the next session, more details came spilling out. She had strove mightily all her young life for the love of her grandfather who raised her after her father abandoned the family shortly after her birth. Her grandfather told her plainly that in order to have a chance at earning his love she would have to "satisfy" him.

The details of the incest and abuse that started when she was a mere four years old came in fits and spurts. Some of the memories were vague. Some of them were specific. There was the time her grandfather took her to a remote location and forced her to dig a shallow grave. Then without a trace of remorse or pity, he told her to bludgeon her pet kitten to death. She only did this under the threat of death using the same method. Then there was the time she asked why her grandfather was so mean to her. He responded by breaking her leg.

It was no surprise to me to learn that her primary manager *part* was called the "pleaser." The pleaser's job was to keep her from being hurt. When she visualized the pleaser, it was a young version of herself with a cast on her leg.

There were other stories too horrible to recount here, and there were many other parts. There were strong *parts* that took over for her when she was under stress allowing her to dissociate entirely, go away to protect yourself. There was an Exile burdened by the horror she had experienced as a child. There was a Firefighter filled with rage that would cut Gwen's flesh in order to make the bad feelings stop.

Despite all this, she sat there with bright eyes and enthusiasm to begin her work. When I began to talk to her about her parts, she looked at me astonished. "How do you know about parts?" she said.

I smiled. "We all have parts. Yours are just a little more distinct and easy to identify than some."

A look of amazed relief swept over her face. "Wow, I thought I was the only one who knew about parts."

When referring to abuse and trauma survivors, therapeutic literature often asks the question, "What if they no longer have a self?" This is the neurological equivalent of saying, "What if they no longer have frontal lobes?" What actually happens to victims of traumatic events is that they are traumatized because they have no internal map of self-in-relationship to fit their experiences. Without that map, a state similar to hypnosis can occur where the person disconnects from the world of the familiar. It is their identity that is challenged, not the *self*. This is similar in some respects to people who go through divorce. It takes a while for them to re-establish their own identity and feel grounded in the world as a single person. This does not mean they have no self or that they cannot self-observe or manage their own reactions or take care of themselves. Judith Herman writes in her excellent book, *Trauma and Recovery*, "The traumatic event thus destroys the belief that one can be oneself in relation to others."

For this reason, trauma and its effects often are trapped in the brain since there is nothing in our experience that can be associated with it. It simply exists in its own frame of reference. Damasio (Descarte's Error) might say that there is no previous dispositional representation whereas Bart Kusko (Fuzzy Thinking) might say there are no habitual tendencies to link such input through the senses. The event is processed, but has no links to any previously established representation of *self*-in-relationship. Just as with hypnosis, the frontal lobes are cognitively disconnected from the emotional content stored in the Limbic System. This explains amnesia, flashbacks, and other seemingly random symptoms of dissociation and post traumatic stress syndrome.

Francine Shapiro, Ph.D., discovered the answer to all of this quite by accident one day. She had been troubled by something and suddenly felt better as she moved her eyes back and forth. What grew out of this discovery, that lateral and diagonal eye movements could produce good feelings, was Eye Movement Desensitization and Reprocessing. EMDR is a revolutionary treatment for PTSD and phobias. In her book on EMDR, Shapiro states that the technique works because " . . . Identity constructs change as imbedded information shifts . . ." In other words, EMDR causes "hidden" information and reactivity about trauma to integrate into our map of *self*-in-relationship-to-the-world. None of this is news to practitioners of NLP, Neuro-Linguistic Programming, who as stated earlier, have long known that eye movements occur in direct relation to neural processing, even when it's out of direct awareness!

Using EMDR, Eye Movement Desensitization Reprocessing, it is not unusual for a rape victim to completely recover from symptoms of PTSD and have an attitude that, "It was awful. It shouldn't have happened. It shouldn't have happened to me, but **this is not about me and my value as a person**. It was a random event and my life will go on."

Judith Herman, on the other hand, uses a technique involving reliving the event or events and mourning them. This is done repeatedly until the emotional content of the trauma has been discharged. This is a much longer process, years as opposed to weeks, but the net effect is the same. EMDR does not always work completely and must be used with reliving techniques similar to those put forth by Herman. The therapeutic aim is to find a way to integrate the trauma into the worldview of those traumatized. Eye movements are a mechanical way of achieving neurological integration at the cognitive level.

For our discussion, it is important to realize that in abuse victims the entire system may be organized around the abuse. Protective Managers may not trust the self enough to lead. The Exile that holds the memories and pain of the events may be hidden and inaccessible. Nevertheless, the IFS, Internal Family Systems, model has been used successfully with these victims. *The Mosaic Mind*, by Goulding and Schwartz is the recounting of the treatment of one such victim, very much like Gwen, who had been incested by her father from age three through age thirteen. In addition, her father had used psychological and physical terror and had involved her in pornography and sex with other men. The story of her internal system is fascinating and ultimately leads to recovery.

A note of caution is appropriate now. We have already talked about self-observation. In the next section, we will give exercises that assist in learning self-leadership and dealing with *parts*. This is always easier and clearer with the help of a qualified therapist, especially one who uses the IFS model. There is certainly nothing wrong with attempting self-observation and the principles of self-leadership. However, the survivor's entire system has evolved to survive the abuse. The Managers that watch over the system are iron willed and in complete control. In these cases, it may take an experienced professional to assist in the healing process.

How to Recognize Parts and Self

As we have said, *parts* are reactive and extreme. It is easy to recognize an Exile when it emerges. Exiles carry the fear, pain, and sadness. When you are experiencing an Exile, you will feel this sadness and pain. A feeling of impending doom is common. Probably you will have a distinctive feeling somewhere in your viscera. Your chest may feel intensely warm or you may get tingles down your back. Paying close attention to these somatic flags and matching them with the feelings that are being experienced will help you recognize a particular *part*.

Like Exiles, Firefighters are easy to spot. If you are waking up with a hangover, your numbing Firefighter may have been activated last night. Any feelings associated with the behavior will help to identify Firefighters. For instance, one person may masturbate when their Exiles flood them with loneliness. Another person may inflict pain on himself or herself to distract from feelings. I know a woman who scrapes her gums until they bleed. She says it is painful, but it also gives her a feeling of ecstasy similar to a sexual experience.

Angry, attacking Firefighters are obvious. If you are angry, you know that a Firefighter is probably rampaging about. Let me qualify this a little. The anger that is over and above what is called for by the situation is Firefighter activity. Let us say that you have been mugged and you are extremely angry. A little rage is probably appropriate in that situation. On the other hand, if you experience that same level of rage when you are turned down for a date, there is Firefighter activation in the anger. This means that the anger is more about your personal history than your present pain.

Notice that there is always a link between Exile pain and Firefighter reactivity. Therefore, if you are beginning to be acquainted with a Firefighter *part*, you need to start looking for the exiled feeling that activates the Firefighter. Let me give you an example. I was having my children to dinner one night. A large salad had been prepared, covered with plastic wrap, and put into the refrigerator for chilling until we sat down. When it was time to eat, my daughter, who was then nineteen, got the salad out and was carrying it to the counter. This was a large, heavy bowl and she tried to do this using only one hand underneath the bowl.

The bowl fell out of her hand onto the hard, tiled floor of the kitchen. The bowl shattered and instantly the entire group became silent. My impulse was to use a four-letter word and to get angry - act out. This would have been Firefighter behavior. Obviously, it was an accident and no attack was directed at me. However, in that instant before my anger rose, I could hear the small voice of an Exile in the back of my mind. "Nobody respects me." To the Exile, the fact my daughter had not been careful with the salad that I had "bought and paid for" was a sign that she did not love or respect me. Of course, this was tied into a major issue of feeling unacceptable.

My awareness of exiled pain of disrespect and how that had triggered my fire fighting anger allowed me to make a choice. For an instant, I knew that my face betrayed the reaction of my Firefighter. But using *self*-leadership, I was able to make another choice. I chose not to say anything. Had I acted out, I would have ruined the rest of the evening. Since I didn't say anything, I was able to stay present and see what had really happened. It seemed that the bowl had done a half flip before it crashed into the floor. What this meant was that the entire salad had landed on the plastic wrap that had covered the top. Nearly all of the salad was salvageable and so was my mood.

As you use *self*-observation increasingly, you will begin to see these relationships between pain and anger or whatever else your Exiles and Firefighters do. The thing to know is the relationship exists. This allows you to begin to search your experience for the linkage between pain and the need to defend against the pain.

What about Managers? Managers are a tougher proposition since one is probably used to passing itself off as your *self*. This particular Manager is probably a high functioning *part*. In other words, to the outside world it looks like you've really got your act together. Nevertheless, if you listen carefully to Managers they tend to be critical and judgmental. Managers are the ones that will spot your Exile in someone else. When you find yourself having a reaction to someone else's way of being in the world, more often than not you are *projecting* your own Exiles into them. Therefore, criticism of others is a clue.

Criticism of yourself is another good clue. How often in your own internal or external dialogue, do you hear imbedded judgments and criticisms about yourself? You are at a restaurant and you order dessert. Then you turn to your friend and say, "I really shouldn't eat this you know. I've got to lose some weight." *Part* of you wants a little comfort food and your Manager *part* is polarized against that *part*. In fact, once you get use to it, you will find that your conversation will contain many shifts from one *part* to another. Managers love to find fault. They also want to please people, often at their own expense. If you find yourself ingratiating yourself to others, you are hearing a Manager. Some Managers will actually try to paralyze others with love, sweetness, kindness, and self-sacrifice. This reminds me of Frank, a client who could do no wrong when it came to his wife. She could not understand why she would get angry at him for his care taking and excessively loving ways. It was simple. His "love" was a way to control her behavior and to feel superior to her.

Manager's behavior is unidimensional. By that, I mean it is not quite real. The act gets old after a while. Do you ever get sick of hearing yourself talk? It's because a Manager is out there fronting for you.

This reminds me of Bernice. When I first met her, I enjoyed listening to her humorous stories. She had worked in a small town and had numerous extremely humorous stories with which she entertained anyone who would listen. Of course, after hearing the stories for the fourth or fifth time it became readily apparent that she was using storytelling as a way to stay away from certain feelings. That explains why afterward I would always feel a little used and uncomfortable. It was obvious that had I been a cardboard character propped up in a corner I would have been just as important to her. All she wanted was an audience. It didn't matter really what I said or did. In a strange way, I wasn't really even there. The relationship did not last.

Another way to look for your Managers is to notice your life-style. Managers are very efficient, smart, competent and in control. Most people are comfortable with their Managers. According to Schwartz, "Managerial *parts* can be very likable, quick, and funny." But remember, they are desperate to maintain a facade of normalcy.

We know people who are driven, achievers, and workaholics. Their lives are out of balance. They do not play. They do not take time for themselves. Possibly, their lives are out of balance because they avoid others by isolating themselves. Some people complain all of the time. Or maybe they are the entertainers of the group, "the life of the party."

Do you have friends who are constantly giving you books or articles that you must read? But if you try to share a good book with them, they will not read it. If you want them to hear something that you have found interesting, they are not likely to participate. They must be right, have to be the source of all knowledge and inspiration, and need constant validation and attention from others to support their intellectual Manager. They do not often "get real," or come to you, and say, "I need your advice or your input on a matter." However, they are always available to give advice.

After a while, you begin to see how "thin" the facade of Managers really is. In my life, I made an amazing discovery. I have a Manager I call "the achiever." He desperately wants my Exile to be accepted and recognized. He strives to earn lots of money, write books, and do speaking engagements. He wants the world to see how wonderful I am. However, this tremendous effort never fulfills the need of the Exile in me. In order to have the acceptance I need, I must let it in. No amount of *doing* will change my way of *being*. The striving of the achiever keeps the world from seeing how wonderful I really am.

Why? This Manager is covering for an Exile that feels totally unacceptable, that shies away from contact with other people, and that carries a lot of pain about not being "much of a person." The achiever Manager's job in my life is to rack up enough credits so that even though "I am not much of a person, maybe people will accept me as an equal because of my achievements." I never realized before discovering this that my drive and ambition was about making me just as good as others!

What about the *self* then? The first thing we can say about the true *self* is that when you are experiencing it, you are not experiencing negative emotions. You feel peaceful, accepting, tolerant, and understanding. If you act out, the *self* understands. It does not mean that you have to like it, but the *self* does not judge the *parts*. The *self* is able to understand the disharmony and polarization of the *parts*.

The *self* might make a statement like, "You know, I really lost my temper yesterday. Although it was inappropriate under the circumstances, it's understandable given my background. Next time I'll try to make a better choice." The *self* knows that you are not your feelings and reactions.

When I was working on my anger, I came to understand that unless I accepted my anger, I would never be able to change. When I lost my temper, I would eventually calm down and say to myself, "Wow! I really lost it. I know this anger is a *part* of me and I accept that. I am open to hearing the message from this *part* of me."

Notice there are no invectives. I am speaking internally to my angry *part* as a *part* of me. The language is not judgmental. I am actively acknowledging that *part* of me, as opposed to disowning it. The more we ignore our *parts*; the louder they scream. So when you experience a strong emotion, sit quietly and address that *part* of you. Say, "Okay, you've got my attention. What do you want to say or want me to hear?"

This kind of awareness is the leadership that comes from the *self*. We are experiencing our Meta-*Self* when we are conscious and free of reactivity. We become patient we understand, and have compassion for others and ourselves.

Chapter Thirteen

Self-Leadership

The success of any work related to our *self* and *parts* hinges on the ability to differentiate our *self* from *parts*. We are not our *parts*. We are not our emotions. We are not our reactions. Although it sometimes seems as if we are only along for a wild ride in our lives, we do not have to assume that all the things that happen are a value judgment about us.

One excellent way to differentiate *self* is to take a little mental trip and leave the *parts* behind. Schwartz, author of *Internal Family Systems Therapy*, recommends this technique, and as simple as it sounds, it is powerful. I will lay out the basics and my interpretation of it, but feel free to modify it. For instance, the technique uses the image of climbing a mountain. I had a client that preferred to visualize setting out to sea.

This exercise assumes that you have some idea of how to identify your *parts*. Close your eyes and picture yourself standing with your *parts* at the base of a mountain. Before you is a path that winds its way up the mountain. You announce to your internal system of *parts* that it is your intention to go on a short journey up the mountain, but that your *parts* are to remain at the beginning of the path while you go on alone. After you make this announcement, pause and sense any feeling that may come up because of this. A *part* or *parts* may object. You will have to take time with each objecting *part* to comfort and reassure them that you will return, that you are not going to abandon them.

When you have addressed the needs of any *part* that objects, turn and start up the path. Stay sensitive to any *part* that may follow. Make sure that they are lovingly but firmly taken back to the waiting area. Finally, after you have dealt with what may have been activated, you are free to move on up the path. Visualize yourself moving up the mountain alone. Take whatever amount of time seems appropriate for this to happen. When you reach the top, take time to experience your self, free of *parts*.

Try to find a vista point that allows you to look down the mountain to where your *parts* are waiting. Feel the feeling of freedom from the reactive system and the closeness you experience to the oneness of the universe or a connection to God depending on your beliefs. Then take whatever time seems appropriate to go down the mountain and become reunited with your *parts*.

Acknowledging Parts

In order to understand how *self* is differentiated from *parts*, you need to acknowledge *parts* when you experience them. By now, you know what to look for. We know our *parts* by the feelings they give us, what they do or how they behave, and their internal voices.

One needs to use awareness to distinguish these things. At a cognitive level, I need to say to myself, "Oh, I really had a reaction there. That was a *part* of me that expresses itself through negative emotion." What is needed is to realize that reactivity is not the Meta-Self. It is a *part* trying to communicate and respond the only way it knows.

Once I have made the distinction between *self* and *part*, I can acknowledge the *part*. This involves saying to myself, "When I feel that feeling, I am experiencing that specific *part*." I must take time to think of other incidents when similar feelings, behaviors, or internal dialogs were present.

When I was working hard on controlling my anger during the time in my life before my awakening experience, I can remember what I would do. When my angry part came up, I would acknowledge it, "Oh, there you go again. What is it you are trying to say to me? What is it you want me to learn," I would try to smile and chuckle to myself. I would send love to my anger. "I know you are angry, but I love myself, and I must love you, my angry part." Acknowledging anger is not the same thing as "acting out" anger. There is an impression these days that we need to "get in touch" with our anger. This too often is used as an excuse to get in someone's face. Accepting our anger does not mean accepting our behavior. By now, I hope it makes sense that change comes through acceptance, not resistance.

Turn inward and notice your feelings and responses. Notice any pictures, dialogs, or sounds that go with the *parts*. Try to locate the *part* in your body, in space, in your mind. Finally, welcome the *part*. It is as if you have discovered a long lost friend. Your friend has been there all of your life, but has constantly been ignored by you. By welcoming the *part* and acknowledging its presence, you are dramatically shifting the system of reactivity. Once a child knows they are no longer going to be ignored, they don't cry so loud. The very act of acknowledging a *part* calms it and changes how it will represent itself in the future.

Denise has an Exile that looks like a smaller version of her. She calls her Exile, "little me." Since she has been able to separate her *self* from that *part*, she talks to "little me" whenever she gets upset. She visualizes the little girl, sees herself holding, hugging, and reassuring that part of her.

Bill has a Manager that is a caretaker. His tendency is to want to "caretake" his wife whenever he thinks she might be upset. After working with and understanding his caretaker, he now notices this habitual tendency and takes the lead by saying, "I understand you want to take care of her so my Exile is not activated. Thank you for trying so hard to help me, but this time I am going to make a different choice."

This really is an exercise in self-observation. It is your job to become increasingly familiar with *parts* and how they represent themselves. Every time you become aware of a *part's* presence in your life, take a second and acknowledge the *part*. *Parts* make their presence known through emotional reactions. Even if it is after the fact, you can still re-experience the *part* and acknowledge it. "I can see how you were trying to deal in that situation." Next, thank the *part*!

Discovering Positive Self-Intention

Since *parts* were created to help us survive, it seems reasonable that they have a positive self-intention. This is hard to see since we have disowned these *parts*. Clearly, Managers have a positive self-intention, but this is not what we see in its style of Managing. Driving toward success is not the intention of an Achiever-type Manager. The Manager is using Achievement to keep us away from pain. Therefore, we need to see the intentions of Managers for what they really are.

As in the example of Bill above, he knows that his caretaking is about his fear. Usually people with caretakers are afraid of conflict. Many caretakers come out of chaotic alcoholic families. Caretaking becomes a matter of personal safety. For Bill, caretaking is an attempt to keep his fear from being activated and fulfill his security needs at the same time. This strategy does not work in Bill's adult life. But the child that created that Manager *part* thought that caretaking was an ideal way of handling the strong reactions of others. In order for Bill to differentiate himself from his protective Manager that wants to caretake, he needs to acknowledge the purpose and value of this *part*. Only in this way can he make other choices.

Similarly, Exiles have positive intentions in our lives. We hate to experience the terror and sadness of our Exiles, but underneath those feelings is a positive self-intention. The same thing applies to Firefighters. It is the way they douse the flames of the Exiles feelings that we do not like. If we search carefully, we will find that Firefighters are fighting a desperate battle for survival. The enormous life force they expend is motivated by positive self-intention.

How do we discover the positive self-intention of *parts*? It is easy. Just sit quietly and ask, "What do you want for my life?" Then listen. The answer will come so fast and clearly that it may surprise you. Typical answers may sound like "To be safe, to get love, to be free," and so forth. Once we understand the positive self-intention of a *part*, it is important to acknowledge it and to thank the *part* for attempting to perform that valuable role in our life.

We must be constantly aware of our *parts'* positive self-intent in spite of their behavior, the feelings, with which they flood us, or the internal voice they may have. The *self* will not be deceived, but will understand this and remain curious about what's really going on. This enables us to respond to the *part*, "thank you for wanting to keep me safe."

Part's Preferred Role

I once had a client who had four *parts*. First, there was an Exiled Little Boy who thought his parents would break up and he would lose them. Second, was the "Old Man." The Old Man was actually a parentified child who liked to isolate him from people. He was a type of Manager. Also, there was another Manager, the Martyr. The Martyr was a pleaser who wanted to avoid conflict and would give him up, make him a doormat, rather than start a fight. Finally, there was an angry teenager, the Firefighter of the group.

After a few weeks of working with these *parts*, I asked what were the preferred roles of the *parts*. In other words, I asked the little boy if he could stop being sad and frightened what he would prefer to do for the person. The response shocked me, "To be part of a family." The little boy *part* wanted to fulfill the person's desire for belonging and to receive love from a group of close people. Instead of expressing pain, the Little Boy *part* represented system resources that would rather put energy into building a "family." Without that opportunity, the person would not have a "family," but would have resources devoted to handling the pain and fear of an out of control childhood.

The Old Man would much rather have been a planner than an isolator. Rather than keeping the person away from people, this *part*, given the choice, would rather have planned grand schemes or a map of the person's life. As long as the Old Man was busy isolating to avoid the Little Boy's pain, the planning resources were diverted to isolating.

The Martyr would have rather been helping others instead of being a "door mat" for everyone else. Pushed into the extreme role of martyr, this *part* used system resources that could have been used in the service of other people.

Finally, and most surprising of all, was the angry teenager. Rather than acting out in rage, this *part* would rather have been working on a cause! The teenager was particularly polarized against the Martyr. The Martyr's "doormat" violations of *self* drove the teenager wild with anger since these violations would activate the Little Boy's pain. The teenager hated the Martyr for this.

When we look at the Exile and Firefighter without their extreme roles, we see affiliation and social consciousness. This is a powerful combination! These powerful system resources were wasted as long as the system remained polarized and forced into extreme roles.

Discovering the preferred roles of *parts* is just as easy as finding their positive intention. "If you weren't driven to achieve acceptance in my life, what would you prefer to be doing for me?" Either suddenly or gradually, the answer for each *part* will be forthcoming. My experience is that it is not hard to discover this once the system's work has started.

Resolving Polarization

In order to resolve polarization, we need to discover which *parts* are polarized with which other *parts*. It is a good bet that Managers hate Firefighters and vice versa. Exiles are usually afraid of Firefighters because they are so powerful and "scary." Firefighters usually are polarized against Managers. As you begin to self-observe, you will hear in your speech and your internal dialogue the reactions of one *part* against another. Once you have identified the polarization, two things need to happen. First, each *part* must be introduced to the other and the positive self-intention of the other revealed. Second, a negotiation must take place to begin to reduce the extreme behaviors. This is a gradual process and cannot happen all at once.

Bill did this using chair work. He imagined his Caretaker in one chair and imagined his angry Firefighter in another. Bill would then ask one or the other a question. Then, in order to answer the question, he would move into the chair that represented that *part* and answer from that *part's* point of view. It turned out that his Caretaker had such an objection to anger that it had been dominating his angry *part* all along. His angry *part* was furious at being suppressed. His angry *part* had been trying to defend his fearful Exile. His Caretaker was afraid that if he let the Anger out that something "not safe" would happen.

Once the Caretaker understood the positive self-intention of the Anger, and the Anger understood the positive self-intention of the Caretaker, things got easier and each was able to come off its extreme position.

Bringing Parts into the Present

As was stated before, Exiles are frozen in the past, usually during a time of abuse, disappointment, abandonment, or some other emotional burdening. Our first problem as *selves* working with our Exiles is to stop their powerful emotions from taking us over. You will need to establish a caring relationship with them, and only allow some of their feelings to come out a little at a time. For this to happen, the *self* must be fully differentiated. The *self* may have to go back in time to nurture the Exiles before they are ready to come to the present to be nurtured.

Before this can happen, it must be established where they are stuck. Most child-like *parts* can give a description or a feeling that helps to orient where they are stuck. The *self* needs to allow the Exile to tell everything it needs to tell about the events of that time. It is then recommended by Schwartz in *Internal Family Systems Therapy*, and some interventions of NLP that the *self* enter the scene to be of help or support in a fashion consistent with the unmet needs of the Exile at that time.

For instance, if a child is being mistreated by a parent, the *self* could ask what resource or assistance the child might need. This could be in the form of imagining the adult *self* stepping in, offering comfort, or confronting the parent. The *self* becomes a surrogate for the power of protection or nurturance that was lacking at that time. In addition, the burden itself needs to be identified. One client described his burden as the torn clothes his Exile wore. The description of the burden is a metaphor for the pain the child *part* carries. Can the burden be left behind so the Exile can move into the present?

This mental journey may need to be made many times before all of the past material has been revealed and all attachment to the burden has been released. It may be necessary, when the Exile is ready to move to a place of safety in the present, to allow a visit to the past on occasion. It is important to prepare a place in the present that allows the Exile time to heal and gain strength.

In the method used by Connirae Andreas in *Core Transformation*, some Exiles are identified in the past as being outside of the body. They are then welcomed into the body of the present *self.*

All of these interventions are metaphorical and allegorical. This is how the brain works. Manipulating neural functions through metaphor means that the networks represented by these metaphors are being changed.

Methods

One of the most powerful methods of doing the work outlined above is called "chair work" or the "empty chair." This technique was used originally in Gestalt therapy. It involves putting out additional chairs to accommodate all of the *parts* with which you might want to work.

First, you sit down in a chair that you have designated for your Meta-Self. Then aloud invite the *part* you want to work with to be present and assign them a chair. You may do this by using a feeling. For instance, the *part* that's angry when you don't get your way. On the other hand, perhaps the *part* makes you procrastinate. Maybe the *part* is the internal critic. Once you have identified the *part*. Ask a direct open-ended question like, "What is the meaning of your anger?" Alternatively, "Tell me about your positive intention for my life." Once you are satisfied that you have asked the question, get up and move to the empty chair. Once you have assumed the new position, speak whatever comes to mind remembering that you are speaking as that *part*.

Should at any time a critical comment be made about that *part*, while you are sitting in the *self*-position, this is an indication that another *part* is talking. What I mean is that if you are sitting in the *self*-position and you start criticizing the *part* represented by the empty chair, this means that a *part* that is polarized is now speaking. Once you become aware of this, you can pull out another chair and sit in it to speak as that critical *part*.

Remember that the *self* is curious, understanding, tolerant, and patient. Any negative or sad emotion that comes up doing chair work is another *part*, usually a polarized *part*.

We can use chair work to address imbalance within the system. Placing *parts* in the empty chairs allows for negotiation and recognition of one *part* by another. One *part* can get larger while another gets smaller. In the previous example of Bill and his Caretaker and Anger, the Caretaker had to become less dominant so that Bill could pay attention to his Anger. It was necessary for his need for self-protection to be balanced with his need to caretake the feelings of others so he didn't feel resentful. The more his Anger felt resentful, the more extreme were the efforts of the Caretaker to suppress the Anger.

Another example I have seen is a playful *part* that is being overwhelmed by an achiever *part*. Chair work allows negotiations to occur to bring balance in how much time is devoted to work vs. play.

Another method involves what Schwartz describes as in-sight. This is making pictures directly in your head. A good way of doing this is to construct a mental room. It can be as simple or as elaborate as your imagination wants. However, it must have a door and a large window. The door allows *parts* to enter and leave the room. The window allows for *parts* observations without contact. This is important when *parts* are afraid or polarized. It allows for observation without direct contact. I always ask permission before asking a *part* to enter the room, meet with or talk to another *part*.

In working with clients, the room approach has been revealing. Often I will put two *parts* in the mental room. I might say, "Now ask them to see if they can work out their differences." I might get a reply like, "Oh, they already have, in fact they want the such and such *part* to come in and work on this too." It is incredible the amount of self-healing that happens once the system understands what going on. When this type of work begins in therapy, *parts* will do a lot of work on their own between sessions.

Another method similar to in-sight is simple internal dialog. We have mentioned examples of this earlier. Often I have had a reaction to something and I will go inside and say, "I see that you have reacted. I understand that your viewpoint is valuable and has worked in the past. Today, I am going to make a different choice. Possibly you can think of other choices that might be available." Another example involves flooding: "I understand you get upset when this happens, but you fill me with so much hopelessness that I become incapacitated. Could you tone it down just a little so I can be more effective?"

One of the most powerful tools I have used is off-handed writing. I first learned of this technique from books by Lucia Capacchione. In *Drawing on the Right Side of the Brain* and *The Power of your Other Hand,* she describes journaling techniques using the non-dominant hand. The way I use this is to ask a question as my *self* with my dominant hand and answer with my non-dominate hand. It is awkward and hard to read and that is the point. While you are using all of your conscious effort to form letters that are legible, the *parts* have an easy time getting their messages into consciousness.

This same effect can be achieved through art. Drawing pictures of messages from *parts* with the non-dominate hand can be quite revealing. Even pictures with the dominant hand contain lots of information. Once I had a client who was a professional artist. I asked her to draw her *parts* for me. She returned with a sketch. It showed three *parts* all on the same page. There was a small picture of a little girl, obviously the Exile. There was a huge picture of a gorgeous woman in elegant southern style clothes, clearly the Manager. And there was a picture of a teenager in slacks reclining, with a smug look on her face.

There was a tremendous amount of information contained in the picture. For one, the teenager's head had a piece of paper over it. I asked what had happened and the client explained that she had made a mistake and had to redraw the face. Later in private, I peeled the patch off the teenager's face. Beneath it was another face with a horribly murderous glare and clenched teeth.

Obviously, what had happened was that the Manager *part* did not like that angry teenager so the face had been redrawn. Here was a metaphor for how the Manager was handling the rage of the Firefighter, the teenager. In addition, the relative sizes of the figures in the sketch showed the balance in the system. Clearly, the Manager was in charge!

Conclusion

This chapter has presented an overview of the techniques and methods of working with *parts*. No workbook, seminar, or therapist can do the work for you. If you are motivated to work with your internal system, there are many ideas presented here to get you started.

This work is much easier and faster with the help of a qualified therapist. Most therapists will be familiar with the techniques mentioned here even if they are not familiar with Internal Family Systems Therapy. The key is to find a therapist whose Manager is not threatened by your knowledge of your own system.

Chapter Fourteen

Eternal Life

Human beings are born with an innate drive toward attachment to a caregiver. One of the many revolutionary ideas presented in this book is that attachment is a superior psychology for understanding humans throughout their lives. Since attachment is primal, it is also fundamental. Our brains, and therefore our behavior, emotions, and metaphorms are all reflexively related to attachment. Attachment is generalized from our first relationship to all intimate relationships. Proximity to our caregiver is generalized to affection. If affection is not present, it is generalized into getting acceptance, recognition, or some other qualitative state of being that means we are okay.

The effects of value judgments generalize attachment. The family system, culture, and life experiences encourage us to split and disown *parts* of ourselves. Since the brain functions in parallel, we are destined to form many different dispositions of self-in-relation or *parts*. Also, since the Limbic System has a sort of neurological priority during childhood and adolescence, our *parts* become reactive, imbalanced, polarized, and without self-leadership.

It is as if we have two shots at life. The first has to do with the effects of value judgments on our neurological structure starting from the attachment phase through childhood. The second starts almost where the first leaves off. Our Neo-Cortex matures late. The Frontal Lobes are pliable from childhood through our teenage years.

The ideas in this book give us a third chance by showing us how to use the Meta-Self that resides in the frontal lobes to provide leadership to the internal system of *parts*. No matter how bad the early years were, we still have the Meta-Self, a powerful force for change in our brains. This book is a road map back to our selves, the redemption of the *self*.

The Harvest of Hate

The apostle Paul wrote a letter to John in which he said that if you hate your brother, you're a murderer. And according to Paul, murders have no eternal life living inside of them (1 John 3:15). Paul seems to be taking things a little far here, doesn't he? What is the difference between all of us *good* people who hate but don't act on it and those who do? There is no fundamental difference. The *part* that hates in me is the *part* that murderers in someone else. That's the point! If we believe that abortion is murder and we hate those who don't agree with us, we have no right to judge who is the worse hater or murderer. If I hate you for abusing your kids, am I a better person than you?

In his award-winning novel, *Ishmael*, Daniel Quinn tells the story of a human who is taught the secrets of life by a wise old gorilla named Ishmael.

Near the end of the story, the human asks Ishmael, "What do I do if I earnestly desire to save the world?"

Ishamel replies, ". . . The story of Genesis must be reversed. First, Cain must stop murdering Abel. This is essential if you're to survive . . . And then, of course, you must spit out the fruit of the forbidden tree. You must absolutely and forever relinquish the idea that you know who should live and who should die on this planet."

It appears that even gorillas know that humankind has turned life over to their collective Limbic System. Each *part* thinks that it is God. Therefore, collectively we think that we are God. The world must conform to our notions of good and evil, blessing and calamity.

The gorilla says, "So. We have a new pair of names for you. The Takers are those who know good and evil, and the Leavers are. . .?"

"The Leavers are those who live in the hand of the gods."

The Tree of Life

That scripture from Paul contained something else unusual. His reference to eternal life "abiding in him" seems to imply that eternal life means much more than just living forever. Throughout sacred writing, we find phrases like *abundant life, everlasting life* that not only imply immortality but a different way of being in the world.

I went back to the Garden of Eden to see if there was a clue that pointed toward this Tree of Life the source of "eternal life." After all, God set up Cherubim and a Flaming Sword to guard the way to the Tree of Life. When I went back to the Hebrew to try and get a better understanding of what God had done, I found that the term "flaming sword" meant magical or enchanted. What happens if we guard the way to Everlasting Life with an enchanted sword or a magical sword?

I mulled this over for a long time. I had seen that the Tree of the Knowledge of Blessing and Misfortune had been a reference to value judgments. If that tree represented value judgments and led to *death*, what did the Tree of Life represent?

Was God playing a little trick? He was using a magical, enchanted sword that flashed everywhere. When we looked at it, we saw something else. Enchanted frogs are princes. Magical sticks turn into snakes. True love awakens a sleeping beauty. The beauty kisses the beast, not because she is in love with the beast, she does it because she sees through the enchantment!

If God wanted to hide the Tree of Life or the path to it, where would he hide it? Where would man be least likely to look? If value judgments require us to look outside ourselves for the evidence of blessing and misfortune, or to split ourselves into *parts* when we see it in our own behavior, then where is the path to Abundant Life?

I believe it is inside of us – the Meta-Self. The enchantment is that we believe that we are our *parts*, our reactivity. If the Limbic System is an allegory for original sin, could the Neo-Cortex and its Frontal Lobes – that self-observing platform in our brains – be an allegory for the path to everlasting or abundant life? I believe so.

Mindfulness

Dr. Martin Luther King, Jr. nominated a poet and Zen master to receive the Nobel Peace Prize. This man's name is Thich Nhat Hanh. I was first introduced to his teaching in the little book, *Peace is Every Step*. This is an adaptation of ancient Buddhist teachings to modern problems. He teaches that each minute, each second of life is a miracle. Mindfulness, then becomes the process of awareness of breathing, of sitting, and walking. Life is a meditation, and it is through mindfulness that we unlock the beauty and power of the moment.

In the book, *The Miracle of Mindfulness*, Hanh talks about mindfulness of the mind or what we have termed the Meta-*Self*. "If you want to know your own mind, there is only one way: to observe and recognize everything about it. This must be done at all times, during your day-to-day life no less than during the hour of meditation."

"While practicing mindfulness, don't be dominated by the distinction between good and evil, thus creating a battle within oneself."

Jesus said that unless we become like little children we would not enter the Kingdom. He also said the Kingdom was at hand.

Mind minding mind, the Meta-Self, is the pathway to Abundant Life. It is the Way to the redemption of our true selves. This is how we overcome the world. The world is the culture of value judgments, but we are to be in the world and not of the world. Mindfulness and self-observation will free us from the world's trap.

Peace and joy are here, in the present moment. *Self* takes us to the present. *Parts* are about the past.

The Self Redeemed

Parts are really about personal boundaries. Reactivity is our instinctive way of knowing something is wrong. Without self-leadership to shine our awareness on this "wrong," we react. The *self*-redeemed will have the traces of that reactivity, but this is a good thing. We need to know when our boundaries have been violated.

A metaphor I use with my clients is that of a box full of reactivity. About 10% of the volume of the box is filled with what I call appropriate reactivity. In other words, we have suffered a boundary violation of some kind: our spouse is overly critical, the boss berates us, we are the victim of an act of violence. Clearly, we are justified to experience some anger, an objection, a reaction to the violation of *self* that occurred.

This 10% of the box gives us just enough awareness that we know that we need to take care of ourselves. This may mean being assertive, or letting the other person know our feelings. "When you said that to me with that tone of voice, I felt devalued and unappreciated."

The other 90% of our box full of reactivity is about our personal history. It is a combination of our Exiles and Firefighters feeling overwhelming pain and lashing out to defend against it. That 90% is the work of therapy or our own work on our *selves*. That 90% is what creates interlocking reactivity among people in relationships, which destroys marriages, careers, and leaves us bewildered about life.

Similarly, the paradoxical strivings of our Manager toward an unattainable goal may eventually be resolved. The taint of that lifestyle will still be there. For instance, I know that my lifestyle is to strive toward recognition that will never come in a form that I can accept. Yet it is that recognition that motivates me to write this book.

If you are a lawyer because it is a civilized way for you to wage your own pathological internal war, healing may not make you a mushroom farmer instead of a lawyer. You may still enjoy the heat of battle in the courtroom. Mindfulness lets you see when the heat is about abusing and punishing instead of righting a wrong or defending a principle. Once the internal system is in balance, one may always have proclivities to be a certain way in the world. However, they will know where their boundaries are and how to do what they do without letting it get out of hand and create imbalance and polarization inside themselves.

Healthy people who are self-aware know their tendencies and do not condemn themselves for them. However, they know that, when they cross the line into reactivity and act out their pain, their lives mean death to self and others. Those who stay within the boundaries of mindfulness can serve their mission to themselves and their fellow man with life giving service.

The Fruit of the Tree of Life is about being fulfilled. That fulfillment spills out to others that you touch. The Fruit of the Knowledge of Good and Evil is death to others and our *selves*. After all our personal work of healing, you may still be a lawyer, a doctor, or a police officer. But you will know where that line between life and death is. Mindfulness lets one stay in the life-giving realm. You are at peace and you experience abundant life.

We all have a long way ahead of us to full *self*-redemption. Self-observation and mindfulness is hard work at first, but it becomes easier with practice. The rewards of living the life we actually can have instead of the one dictated to us by our *parts* is worth the sacrifice.

Many years ago, I heard an audiotape by Marianne Williamson, the author of many personal growth books. She told a story about a meeting that she was to attend. She knew before hand that one of the people there was going to be a woman who Marianne really didn't care for much. Before entering the meeting, she said a silent prayer. As I recall it went like this, "Lord, let me see this situation another way."

This openness led Marianne to a completely different experience with this woman, one that was new, and emotionally satisfying. Since hearing that tape, I have tried this same method nearly every time I go into a new situation. It puts me into a place of expectancy rather than prejudice. I have seen miracles as a result.

Epilogue

Rick is sitting in front me telling me how things have been going since he left therapy a few weeks ago. He's excited about his new life. He's telling me about his relationship with his girlfriend and how it's changed since he has had so many new insights.

Rick came to see me some time ago at the urging of his girlfriend. It seemed he was cold, remote, discounting, and generally hostile. When his girlfriend wanted to talk about her feelings, he would usually put her down and disconnect emotionally.

It didn't take too many sessions for us to uncover his Exile. When he was a small boy, at about the age of five his parents divorced. It was a hostile, bitter, chaotic divorce - the worst kind for a child. All of a sudden in the middle of everything, his mother packed up all their belongings and flew him and his sister across the country from the East Coast to California. He didn't see his father again for over 12 years.

In his child's mind he was sure the reason that he no longer saw his father was because some how he was unacceptable to his father. This left a void in his life that he filled with a Manager *part* that was extremely high functioning and industrious and that could "take care of himself." This self-reliant Manager caused him to be quite successful in business. But as we have seen in this book, the real purpose behind this self-reliance was to stay away from those feelings of unacceptability. Naturally, whenever that Exile would escape he would get particularly angry and hard to be with. It was as if he would reject other people before they rejected him.

Rick's work in therapy actually took a very short time. Once he realized that his lifestyle and his emotional reactions were linked to those early experiences rather than what was happening to him in the present, it was as if he had a new lease on life.

Suddenly he could see his girlfriend's exile, and this explained all of her behavior. He realized that she was fear based - desperately afraid of being abandoned. This wasn't because of any particular trauma in early life. The genesis of her Exile was the fact that her father had traveled extensively as a salesperson and when he was home, he was busy with business matters. Consequently, he never really spent a lot of time with her. Therefore, she was desperate for that emotional connection. She was afraid that if she didn't connect emotionally with her father that her father would leave her. And of course he did. Every Monday morning he was back on the road and she was left with that sense of abandonment.

Once Rick saw this clearly, it explained her clinging behavior and her temper tantrums. Rick was able to overcome his feelings of unacceptability, which he knew were not personal about her. That enabled him to move into her fear and take care of her, giving her the emotional connection she so desperately needed. She responded with appreciation that made him feel more acceptable. The cycle of conflict had been broken.

Rick, however, was able to apply these insights and new awareness to many other areas of his life. Suddenly he gained a new appreciation for the behavior of his business clients, his friends, and his family. As he sat there, I could see he had a new sense of power and freedom. The old tendencies were still there, but he knew he was the master of his internal system. He was in the lead. His behavior, his emotions, and his assumptions about other people had radically changed. He knew and was able to take responsibility for his own personal process. Often times he was able to do this in the dynamics of the moment without going directly to those reactions that represented his personal history. This gave him new freedom to choose different behaviors, make different assumptions, and operate on the world as opposed to letting the world operate on him.

As I watched him walk out the door and down the steps to the parking lot, I remembered many other clients that had gone through the same "right of passage" in their personal growth work. I hoped that I would see Rick again, since the initial breakthroughs are so powerful they forget that they must still achieve balance, harmony, and self-leadership in their internal system of *parts*. Each *part* needs to be worked with to bring them into the present so that the constraints that hold those powerful resources can be released.

For now, it was clear that Rick could see that his emotional reactivity was related to the past as opposed to the present. That insight alone and the new awareness that comes with it is the doorway to freedom. Rick was now free to be in relationship to the world using his Meta-Self.

As he opened his car door, he looked up at me and waved. I could tell by the tremendous change in him that he had walked through the doorway to freedom and that the Tree of Life lay directly in his path.

Afterward:

My Moment of Enlightenment

"My God," I shouted. "I take everything personally!" What had she been saying that had triggered such a sudden pronouncement? The tone of my voice had a sound of disbelief for a moment. I felt like the guy in the cartoon when the proverbial light goes on. It was a revelation, some form of serendipity. I don't really know how to describe it. It was as if a *part* of me, long dormant, had suddenly been awakened with a strange insight. I had the ability to stand aside like a third person and to comment on my own behavior. When I moved to that perspective, it was suddenly so obvious that I couldn't contain my shock.

What had Kathy been saying that triggered such a spontaneous shift in consciousness? Kathy and I had been together for some time, and I had become quite attached to her. I remembered that she had been talking about her friend, Carol. Carol was a workaholic, a compulsion that made friendship nearly impossible. Kathy called Carol her best friend, and yet every time they arranged to get together, Carol would pull the plug at the last minute because of work obligations. Still, Kathy loved Carol and would refuse to criticize or cut her off.

We had been talking about some upcoming social event to which Carol was invited to bring her boyfriend. I had been listening to all of this with a growing agitation. If Carol was so unreliable, why have her as a friend? She had constantly disappointed Kathy. I cared for Kathy, and, by God, I would have no one treat her like that. If Carol couldn't learn to treat Kathy better, who needed her? Why even go out of the away to invite her? The outcome was always the same - disappointment, rejection, hurt. I was angry just thinking about it. I wanted to defend Kathy against further disappointment.

I guess that's when it hit me. Kathy had been arguing with me. She was going in no way to give up Carol. She expressed her affection for Carol and talked about the years they had been friends. I barely listened. I was having my own internal dialog grinding away inside fuming. That's when it happened. I stopped and looked at Kathy. She was a little perturbed, but at me not Carol. I was worked up, defensive, and ready to fight.

That's when it hit me. *My reactions were about me*, not Kathy. It was as if Carol had been *abandoning me, screwing me, and letting me down*. I was feeling both hurt and angry. In this moment of instant clarity, I could see what I had been doing. That's when I interjected, "I take everything personally!"

Later I would learn that that simple statement began to describe what was really happening inside of me. At that particular moment, I could see some of my internal process and come up with a descriptive phrase. My reaction, my anger was about me, not about Kathy and Carol. It was *my* hurt, *my* sense of abandonment, *my* unmet emotional needs. But earlier I hadn't seen all of that. I only saw that somehow, in a bizarre way, Kathy had become me and I had entered into the picture as if Carol were intentionally hurting, disappointing me. She couldn't treat me that way! I'd show her! I'd cut her off, refuse to take her telephone calls. Let her suffer. Let her find out what was like to have no one care about you, to be let down, and disappointed. She can't do this to me!

Before my awakening insight, I couldn't see that it was a totally inappropriate response. Kathy needed my support. She cared deeply for her friend, and I needed to respect that. My confusing my reactions with Kathy's reactions had put me in an emotional state that was not called for. It also did something else that I would discover years later. It made Kathy invisible. By interpreting her comments through the lens of my own reactions, I was making her a non-person in the conversation. Did she feel heard or understood by me? I would have no way of knowing. I wasn't even in the room! I had become Kathy. Carol had become everyone who had ever let me down. And I was off in space. Strong body chemicals and hormones were flooding through me. I was reliving hurt and pain from somewhere out of my awareness. I was in a self-induced trance and probably incapable, at that time, of responding in any other way.

Somehow, I had a flash of insight. A small one to be sure, but one that would trigger years of growth and personal work. Even so, for a fraction of the second, I was able to "see" what I was doing. I was "taking everything personally."

A Few Hours of Peace That Passes Understanding

What happened next shocked me even more. It's hard to describe. I was in a state of clarity like none I had ever experienced. There was a sense of timelessness. As I uttered those words of personal revelation, my understanding and perspective were transformed.

In some respects, it was similar to the sensation one gets when reading a book that forces your fingers too swiftly turn page after page. After all, the author had written words and words only. Nevertheless, through our own senses, we construct a world as real and vivid as the one we perceive around us.

This was no fantasy. It felt like a meta-reality that had always been there. In an instant, I could literally see the thread of the pain of "taking things personally" back through time, interwoven throughout my entire life. It had been there affecting almost everything I had done, my motivations, my movements. I had thought that I moved through life independently. Not so! This internal process had bumped me this way and that. So much of what I had done and the way I had lived was a reaction to this "taking things personally."

What did this really mean? How had this threat of internal pain manifested itself in my life?

I could see how my drive to achieve had given me kind of a "chip on the shoulder" determination. "I'll show you!" My pain had distilled into a simmering anger that drove me forward to make sure they, whoever they were, would know me, would be forced to reckon with me.

This was also woven through my career choice. It had been the motivation behind the books and articles. In fact, all of my life's accomplishments had an edge of anger, responding to pain. Personal pain was the fuel that ran my life. Each new situation was another way of expressing the same pain response. Sure, life's circumstances looked different. One time it was a job. On an earlier occasion, it had been athletics. Then there was a period in my life when I was active in church. My anger even colored my religious participation. As a young adult, much of what had driven my failed attempt to run for public office had been fueled by this need to overcome some imaginary, cosmic put down.

That's not to say I didn't achieve my goals. I made money in business. I had books published. I was even proud of some of my work. The things that happened in my life weren't bad or corrupt. They just had a slight taint. My life looked successful. The small bit of impurity was barely discernible in the end product. Like a horse being ridden with spurs, the pain of taking life so personally had repeatedly jabbed me in the flanks. Keeping the dark side of myself under control had given me a persistence to keep galloping, but charging further into the darkness of "making something happen" instead of being fully alive.

Somehow, this deep wound had become insidious in my life. It appeared I had freedom of choice. It appeared that I had chosen this or that path on my own with a clear head. But this is not what really had happened at all.

I realized in this instant of metaphysical mercy that I was asleep, sound asleep, pretending to be awake. I could stay asleep by making decisions out of my pain and anger. It was a way of administering anesthetic. If I slept soundly enough, I wouldn't feel the pain. To awaken meant one thing. I had to deal with the fact that I took things personally and that this trait had robbed me of freedom and the true experience of joy itself.

To say I was astonished by all this is an understatement. I was left with a profound sense of wonderment - of awe. Even that feeling could not compare to what was to happen. I was about to experience a new feeling; A feeling I had never felt before. I now call it the peace "which passeth all understanding" (Phillippians 4:7). However, all I knew then was that the next morning dawned like none I had ever known. It was gorgeous. The sun was bright in a cloudless sky. I had opened my eyes to a New World.

How shall I describe it? There was nowhere to go nothing to do. I didn't need to accomplish anything. I knew deep to the core that all I was called upon to do was to simply *be*. I know how simplistic that must sound. It reminded me of the passage in Ray Bradbury's *the Martian Chronicles* where he talks about how the Martians had discovered the secret to life as the pure enjoyment of *being*. The experience I had was very similar to the Tantra concept of bliss.

The idea of just *being* was foreign to me. Up until that moment, I had been a driven man. I was now fully aware that there was nowhere to go, nothing to do, and nothing to accomplish. It was enough that I was alive and in the moment. To put this simply, it was a pleasure being alive. I felt like an inheritor of everything that God wanted me to have. In addition, I didn't fear death. If my life ended the next day, it wouldn't have mattered to me. The aliveness I felt in the moment was fulfilling. It was clear to me that there was nothing to fear. Life was not a fearful place. I was fully enveloped in love and a peace that I knew had not been bestowed upon me from the outside, *it had welled up from inside of me*.

Fear, anger, and pain had covered my peace. My peace had been there all along. I was sure that my natural state was one of profound peace. Somehow, in my life, I had learned to block this peace and had added layer after layer of negative emotionalism until my natural sense of peace had been stamped out.

That moment of my enlightenment had the effect of peeling back those ugly layers exposing the core of my being. I felt completely fulfilled in the moment, sufficient in and of myself.

Over the next few days, this feeling gradually left. I mourned the loss of it as fear and pain and anger crept back to dominate my thoughts. However, in those hours of clarity, my life was changed forever.

Another Thread is Found

The thread of pain weaving through my life was not the only thing I saw. There was another thread. A hunger to know the meaning of life and to reveal it to others. While I had been busy accomplishing, achieving and, proving, I had also been busy nurturing my true hunger. I had studied everything I could find about human potential. My seeking had taken me to religion, both Eastern and Western, hypnosis, Nero linguistic programming, goal setting, affirmation's; anything that might unlock human potential.

This hunger for knowledge and answers had been a strong force in my life. I always kept coming back with an intense yearning to learn, to know, and help others experience their full potential.

During those precious hours of clarity, I vowed to bring this piece of my soul out into the open. It deserved a prominent place in my life. I had never considered becoming a therapist, counselor, or anything of the kind. It didn't fit my image of the "successful" person I was driven to be. But, I made a conscious commitment to honor what I could glimpse of my core self. It took over a year for the timing to be right to begin the exploration of that part of me. It was then that I enrolled in graduate school to study Marital and Family Therapy.

I tried to do this differently than I had done anything else in my life, with no end goal in mind. I wanted the experience - to immerse myself in the process of being. I intentionally did not set up expectations or look forward to anything. I wanted to do something for once in my life and to allow myself to experience it fully.

In the process, I learned about myself, about life, and about how things work. I discovered something I never thought I would. Doing the work of therapy, I experienced fulfillment and discovered deep meaning in my life.

That is the point of this book. Each of us has a place inside of us where we are sure of ourselves and our place in the world. When we are that real authentic self, we are fulfilled. It is our true human potential, the full inheritance of what life has to offer. We need to learn how to work through our own paradox that is blocking our true selves from being fully empowered. When you grasp the meaning of this paradox, you will immediately see your potential, and move forward into its expression. I invite you to join me in this discovery.

About Mark Waller

PROFESSIONAL PROFILE:

Mark Waller is an award winning author of four books and numerous articles. A licensed Marriage and Family Therapist, he has been a management consultant for over ten years and has conducted workshops for manufacturers, utilities, and the computer industry. He has lectured at the University of Wisconsin and George Washington University. Mark has a B.A. in Business, a Masters Degree in Counseling, and a Ph.D. in Psychology. He has extensive experience helping executives and couples, as well as groups.

Mark is a highly respected clinician and professional with a worldwide reputation for his interpersonal and communications skills. He is a demonstrated leader and innovator who is a professional platform speaker/trainer and has a proven track record of achievement in sales and marketing.

PERSONAL PROFILE:

Mark Waller had a midlife crisis and became a statistic. At 40, he was a successful technical consultant, and the author of three books on computers and electrical power. His first book was entitled *Computer Electrical Power Requirements*. His second book, *PC Power Protection*, was a Tab Book Club main selection. His third book, *Mark Waller's Harmonics*, established him as an acknowledged leader in the field of electrical power quality. He received The Award of Achievement from the Society of Technical Communications in the 1988–89 competition for an article written for *Byte Magazine*. At that time, he was named a "Finalist" in L. Ron Hubbard's "Writers of the Future" contest (he is not a Scientologist). He traveled the country giving workshops and consulting for companies such as Southern California Edison and The Jet Propulsion Laboratory. He taught classes at Georgetown University and the University of Wisconsin.

Then disaster struck. The economy, the marriage, and the lifestyle all

Mark Waller, Ph.D.

collapsed at the same time. Mark had nothing left but pain and fear. During this dark night of the soul Mark experienced an *awakening*. This led to a career and life change. His next book, THE DANCE OF THE LION AND THE UNICORN, was born from new insight that followed.

Today Mark is a Licensed Marriage and Family Therapist in Southern California where he lives with his wife Sheila. His passion is helping others experience *awakening* as well.

Reader Survey

Please circle one answer.

Did you enjoy *BEYOND THE PARADOX OF BEING HUMAN*? Yes   No
Please explain why or why not _____
_____
_____

Was it helpful?   Yes   No
Did you learn anything new?   Yes   No
Could you relate it to your own life or experience?   Yes   No
Did it make you want to take action?   Yes   No

What was your favorite part or concept? _____
_____
_____

Do you have any additional comments? _____
_____
_____

Would you be willing to write a review to be posted on Amazon.com? If so please go to their site and look up my book. Links for review submission are clearly posted. Thank you very much!

Can we add you to our e-mail newsletter list? Please print legibly.

_____

Would you like to be notified when Mark Waller comes to your area for a workshop or book signing? *Please make sure you give us your e-mail address.*

_____   Yes   No

Please fill out and mail to: Or scan and e-mail as an image file to:
Mark Waller   mail@markwaller.com
4195 Chino Hills Pkwy PMB 611   For more information go to
Chino Hills, Ca 917098   www.markwaller.com

www.ingramcontent.com/pod-product-compliance
Lightning Source LLC
Chambersburg PA
CBHW031207270326
41931CB00006B/455